Causal Factors in American Economic Growth in the Nineteenth Century

Prepared for
The Economic History Society by

PETER TEMIN

Professor of Economics,
Massachusetts Institute of Technology

First published 1975 by
THE MACMILLAN PRESS LTD
London and Basingstoke
Associated companies in New York Dublin
Melbourne Johannesburg and Madras

SBN 333 17087 3

Printed in Great Britain by
THE ANCHOR PRESS LTD
Tiptree, Essex

For Charlotte

STUDIES IN ECONOMIC AND SOCIAL STUDIES

This series, specially commissioned by the Economic History Society, provides a guide to the current interpretations of the key themes of economic history and social history in which advances have recently been made or in which there has been significant debate.

Originally entitled 'Studies in Economic History', in 1974 the series had its scope extended to include topics in social history which are closely related to studies in economic history, and the new series title 'Studies in Economic and Social History' signalises this development.

The series gives readers access to the best work done, helps them to draw their own conclusions in major fields of study, and by means of the critical bibliography in each book guides them in the selection of further reading. The aim is to provide a springboard to further work rather than a set of pre-packaged conclusions or short-cuts.

ECONOMIC HISTORY SOCIETY

The Economic History Society, which numbers over 3000 members, publishes the *Economic History Review* four times a year (free to members) and holds an annual conference. Inquiries about membership should be addressed to the Assistant Secretary, Economic History Society, Peterhouse, Cambridge. Full-time students may join the Society at special rates.

STUDIES IN ECONOMIC AND SOCIAL HISTORY

Edited for the Economic History Society by M. W. Flinn

Contents

Note on References

Name and date references within square brackets in the text relate to works listed in the Sources Cited section of the Bibliography; page numbers, where appropriate, are printed in italic, e.g. [Lebergott, 1964, *510*].

Editor's Preface

SO long as the study of economic and social history was confined to a small group at a few universities, its literature was not prolific and its few specialists had no great problem in keeping abreast of the work of their colleagues. Even in the 1930s there were only two journals devoted exclusively to economic history and none at all to social history. But the high quality of the work of the economic historians during the inter-war period and the post-war growth in the study of the social sciences sparked off an immense expansion in the study of economic history after the Second World War. There was a great expansion of research and many new journals were launched, some specialising in branches of the subject like transport, business or agricultural history. Most significantly, economic history began to be studied as an aspect of history in its own right in schools. As a consequence, the examining boards began to offer papers in economic history at all levels, while textbooks specifically designed for the school market began to be published. As a specialised discipline, social history is an even more recent arrival in the academic curriculum. Like economic history, it, too, is rapidly generating a range of specialist publications. The importance of much of the recent work in this field and its close relationship with economic history have therefore prompted the Economic History Society to extend the scope of this series – formerly confined to economic history – to embrace themes in social history.

For those engaged in research and writing this period of rapid expansion of studies has been an exciting, if rather breathless one. For the larger numbers, however, labouring in the outfield of the schools and colleges of further education, the excitement of the explosion of research has been tempered by frustration arising from its vast quantity and, frequently, its controversial character. Nor, it must be admitted, has the ability or willingness of the academic historians to generalise and summarise marched in step with their enthusiasm for research.

The greatest problems of interpretation and generalisation have tended to gather round a handful of principal themes in economic and social history. It is, indeed, a tribute to the sound sense of economic and social historians that they have continued to dedicate their energies, however inconclusively, to the solution of these key problems. The results of this activity, however, much of it stored away in a wide range of academic journals, have tended to remain inaccessible to many of those currently interested in the subject. Recognising the need for guidance through the burgeoning and confusing literature that has grown around these basic topics, the Economic History Society hopes in this series of short books to offer some help to students and teachers. The books are intended to serve as guides to current interpretations in major fields of economic and social history in which important advances have recently been made, or in which there has recently been some significant debate. Each book aims to survey recent work, to indicate the full scope of the particular problem as it has been opened up by recent scholarship, and to draw such conclusions as seem warranted, given the present state of knowledge and understanding. The authors will often be at pains to point out where, in their view, because of a lack of information or inadequate research, they believe it is premature to attempt to draw firm conclusions. While authors will not hesitate to review recent and older work critically, the books are not intended to serve as vehicles for their own specialist views : the aim is to provide a balanced summary rather than an exposition of the author's own viewpoint. Each book will include a descriptive bibliography.

In this way the series aims to give all those interested in economic and social history at a serious level access to recent scholarship in some major fields. Above all, the aim is to help the reader to draw his own conclusions, and to guide him in the selection of further reading as a means to this end, rather than to present him with a set of pre-packaged conclusions.

M. W. FLINN
Editor

University of Edinburgh

1 Introduction

THE study of American economic history has been revolutionised in the past twenty years. Starting from the work of Kuznets [1952], far more data about the American economy in the nineteenth century have been collected than was believed possible only a few years ago. And starting essentially from the work of Conrad and Meyer [1958], an increasing number of explicitly formulated hypotheses have been tested using these data. The distinguishing feature of the so-called New Economic History is just this juxtaposition of explicitly formulated hypotheses and historical data.

This book is an introduction to the new literature as it pertains to American economic growth in the nineteenth century. The new data will be surveyed and several of the hypotheses that have been advanced to explain them will be examined. In addition, the impact on economic growth of several institutions prominent on the American scene will be discussed.

Because the use of explicit hypotheses and models is the most striking aspect of this work, the present study concentrates on it. (Readers interested in the sources of the data are referred to the Cited Sources.) One cannot present the conclusions that emerge from these models without a taste of the reasoning behind them, since the conclusions cannot be evaluated without an understanding of the methodology used to derive them. A few articles therefore have been selected for extensive discussion, and the limitations of space have been interpreted as limitations on the number of such descriptions as opposed to the length of each. The articles chosen are both important and amenable to analytic summary. The discussion here will be highly critical in order to show the reader the kinds of questions that should be raised about even the most tightly reasoned piece, but the criticisms should not be allowed to obscure the enormous contribution to our historical understanding made by these important articles.

2 The Measurement of Growth

THIS survey is concerned with recent research into the nature of economic growth in the United States. One of the first tasks in the analysis of growth is its measurement, and this survey begins with that.

Economic growth means different things to different people, but most of the work considered here has used one of two alternative definitions. Growth may be represented by changes in the size of national income, or by changes in the size of national income per capita. The latter is the more usual definition, and this discussion will be organised around it. First of all, however, a description of the growth of the American population is needed to provide a connection with discussions of total national income.

Population grew rapidly in the United States for approximately a century following the Declaration of Independence. It then slowed down gradually – and a bit unevenly – to its present very modest rate of increase. The rate of growth of population before 1870 was about 3 per cent a year. It averaged about 2 per cent for the rest of the nineteenth century and fell to less than 1 per cent during the Depression of the 1930s. Population growth then speeded up again briefly before falling back again below the level of the 1930s.

The high rate of population growth was produced by the combination of a rapid rate of natural increase and immigration. Both can be regarded as in part the results of the high standard of living – produced in turn by the high national income per capita – of the United States. At any moment of time, the high rate of natural increase was the most important component of this change; the growth of population by immigration averaged only about 0·5 per cent a year throughout the nineteenth century. As a result, the proportion of foreign-born people in the United States never rose above 15 per cent of the population. This is one way to view the problem, but it is not the best way. It examines only the direct effect of immigration on population size and neglects the fact that immigrants contributed indirectly to the growth of population by having children. For, while relatively few Americans were actually born abroad, essentially all Americans were the descendants of immigrants. If there had been no immigration after 1790, and if the rate of natural increase of people already in America had been the same as it actually was, the population in 1920 (when immigration was curtailed sharply) would have been only half as large as it actually was [Easterlin, 1972].

Turning now to the question of national income – or its equivalent, national product – per capita, the historian can rejoice in a happy accident. The Constitution of the United States requires that there be a census of the United States every ten years, in order to allocate seats in the House of Representatives. Now, a simple count of population by location would have been enough to do this. The various people who took the census, however, tried to get more information, and the census grew over time from something approximating a population count to the vast collection of data that is now called the United States Census.

Some data on economic activity were collected for 1810, 1820 and 1840, but it was not until the Census of 1850 that a systematic attempt was made to collect and synthesise data on manufacturing in the United States. A new census law was passed for the Census of 1850 which provided for the collection of data, but the appropriation (i.e. the allocation of funds) did not keep pace with the needs of the data and the full Census was never published. (It can, however, be found in Congressional documents for 1859.) This law – with better appropriations – remained in force for the Censuses of 1860 and 1870 also, and a new law covered the Census of 1880. At this time, specialists were hired to collect data on specific industries, special reports were commissioned on topics of interest, and the whole scope of the census was enlarged. By 1880, therefore, one can begin to speak of the 'modern' census.

The census data form the starting point for any investigation into the growth of national income in the United States. They are far better than the British data for the same period, but they still have many problems. Historians have estimated differently the distance down the tunnel of history illuminated by them. Martin [1939] used these and other data to provide estimates of national income every decade from 1790 to the 1930s. Recent work has cast doubt upon both his methods and the reasonableness of his conclusions for the early nineteenth century, and subsequent investigators have been more cautious [Kuznets 1952; Parker and Whartenby 1960]. The more recent research stems more from the work of Kuznets, recently honoured by a Nobel Prize in economics, than from Martin.

Kuznets thought that the census was not a reliable guide before 1880. He therefore extended his estimates of the national product back to 1870, on the basis that the earlier census was complete enough to extrapolate back for one additional decade before 1880 but no more [Kuznets, 1952].

Gallman [1966] enlarged and extended Kuznets's series by making use of the censuses from 1850 to 1870. As our experience with these data has grown, so has our confidence in our ability to wrest a reliable story out of them. Gallman's series, like Kuznets's, was extended back one decade before the advent of reliable data by using the less reliable preceding Census of 1840 for extrapolation. Intercensal years were interpolated by a variety of means too complex to be described here, and the result was a series of real national product from 1835 onwards.

The data compiled in this fashion show that economic growth was continuing rapidly after 1840. Gross domestic product per capita in constant prices rose at an annual rate of about 1·5 per cent for the remainder of the century (see Table 1, page 17 below). (This is the same order of magnitude as the growth rate of British per capita product.) But was it also taking place before that time? Rostow [1960] followed a trend among historians when he assigned the American 'take-off' to the years just following 1840, but recent research has cast doubt on the idea that the economy – as distinct from the availability of our data – changed sharply in 1840.

David [1967] projected Gallman's estimates of the national product back to 1800 on the basis of the demographic evidence collected in the early nineteenth century. He did this by means of two assumptions. First, he noted that the output per worker in non-agricultural activities was about double that in agriculture in 1840, and he assumed that this ratio stayed constant for the forty years before then. Since the proportion of the labour force engaged in agriculture fell from 83 per cent in 1800 to 63 per cent in 1840, this change alone made for a rise in per capita output. (The labour force was not observed directly, since the Census of 1800 did not ask the relevant questions; it was estimated from data on the location and on the age structure of the population.)

We do not have data on agricultural output for most of this period, but it is hard to believe that it fell. All the indirect evidence suggests instead that the per capita consumption of foodstuffs and the provision of crops to industry rose or at worst stagnated during these years. Since agricultural imports were negligible, it follows that production per capita did not fall. Accordingly, David's second assumption was that agricultural output per head of the total population stayed constant from 1800 to 1840. This apparently innocuous assumption has far-reaching consequences, since a declining proportion of the population was engaged in agricultural activities. (Remember that this is inferred from the census observation that a declining proportion of the population lived in rural areas.) It follows that the output of each agricultural worker was rising. Per head of the population, fewer workers were required to produce the same output.

David concluded that per capita income was rising before 1840 for two reasons. There was a gain as workers left agriculture for other occupations, and there was a gain as workers in agriculture became more productive. (Here and elsewhere in this survey I have neglected some of the fine points of David's argument in which he refines the analysis beyond the limits shown here.) The speed with which income rose, he found, was not very different from the speed with which it rose after 1840.

These conclusions raise a variety of questions. First, how good are the assumptions on which the extrapolation was based? There is no way of testing the first assumption directly since the relevant data for the period do not exist. Data for later periods, however, suggest that this is a relatively stable ratio and the conclusions based on them appear firm. The second assumption synthesises a variety of historical evidence collected for reasons unrelated to the production of estimates of national income. Without asserting that this assumption is completely valid, the burden of proof is now on the historian who asserts the contrary. In addition, if per capita income was rising from 1800 to 1840, the rise in income would have produced an increase in per capita consumption of agricultural commodities and the assumption may well understate the magnitude of the efficiency gain in agriculture.

Secondly, where did all those workers who left agriculture go? Most people guess manufacturing, but less than 10 per cent of the labour force was occupied in manufacturing in 1840 [Lebergott, 1964, *510*]. Most of these workers therefore must have gone into the other large sector of the economy: services. We know far less about this sector, particularly in this early period, than we would like. Some of the new service workers must have been domestic servants in the growing cities. Many of them were engaged in commercial and transport activities. To the extent that workers were being transferred from agriculture to commerce and related activities rather than to manufacturing, it would be more correct to speak of a *commercial revolution* than an industrial revolution for this period. This is an intriguing idea, and one we know all too little about.

A third question is this: economic growth appears to have been a familiar process by 1840; was this also true in 1800? The answer, to the best of our knowledge, appears to be 'no'. Assume that David's assumptions hold true for the period before 1800 as well as the years thereafter. What do we find? Most of the labour force was in agriculture in 1800. (More accurately, most people lived in rural areas in 1800.) There might have been a larger proportion in agriculture during the eighteenth century, but the proportion could not have been very much larger. Some people were needed even before the industrial revolution to produce manufactured goods and perform services. The gains achieved by transferring workers out of agriculture accordingly were small before 1800. By the same token, David's second assumption does not indicate the presence of per capita growth before 1800. The proportion of the population engaged in producing agricultural goods did not change very much, and an assumption that per capital agricultural output remained constant therefore implies that productivity in this sector did not change much either. This line of argument suggests that the growth of per capita income observed for the nineteenth century was not a characteristic of the eighteenth century.

Table 1

Growth in the U.S. Private Domestic Economy
Average Annual Growth Rates
(Percentages)

	1800–55	1855–1905	1905–27	1927–67
Real gross product	4·2	3·9	3·3	3·2
Per capita real output	1·1	1·6	1·7	1·8
Labour input per capita	0·6	0·5	−0·3	−0·9
Output per unit of labour input	0·5	1·1	2·0	2·7
Output per unit of total input	0·3	0·5	1·5	1·9

Source : Abramovitz and David [1973, *430*].

The basic facts of what we can now label nineteenth-century growth can be summarised as shown in Table 1. Our argument so far has given reason to distinguish the nineteenth century from earlier years; this table gives reasons to distinguish it also from later years. Gross domestic product in real terms (i.e. in constant prices) rose more slowly in the twentieth century than in the nineteenth. But population also grew more slowly, and per capita output rose more rapidly in the later period than in the earlier, although the difference was not large between 1855 and 1905 and 1905 and 1927.

More important than these variations was a change shown only indirectly in Table 1. People worked long and increasing hours in the nineteenth century, and they worked increasingly less in the twentieth. The result was that the work expected from a given worker in 1900 was much greater than the work expected either in 1800 or in 1967. (We are talking of inputs, of course, not outputs.) This movement, in combination with the slow-down of population growth, produced the change shown in the third line of Table 1. The labour input to the economy rose relative to the population in the nineteenth century; it fell in the twentieth. As a result, the output per unit of labour input rose far more rapidly in the twentieth century than it did in the nineteenth. Taking the growth of the capital stock into account, we find that this conclusion holds true for the output per unit of total input as well, as the final line of Table 1 shows. Approximately 90 per cent of the growth in gross domestic product in the nineteenth century is explained by growth in the factors of production, but these factors only account for about half of the growth after 1900. Alternatively, the growth of conventional factors of production account for over two-thirds of the growth of real per capita product in the nineteenth century, but less than 10 per cent of the per capita growth since then.

This period includes the American Civil War (1861–5), of course, but the impact of the war is not visible in the table. An earlier view of the war, which saw it as an initiating event in economic growth, has been replaced by the view that it was an interruption to growth. The primary impact of the Civil War, in other words, was not to spark technological progress or the reorganisation of American industry; it lay rather in the temporary absence from the economy of labour, capital, and foreign exchange earned by the export of cotton [Cochran, 1961; Gilchrist and Lewis, 1965; Engerman, 1966].

We should not jump from here to the assertion that there was no technical change in the nineteenth century and that the Industrial Revolution was all a myth. Many events not shown in Table 1 were taking place. They all had their effects on the magnitudes shown in the table, but this table is a pale reflection of history. Two phenomena may be mentioned here; the following chapters in this survey will expose many more to view.

To discover our first phenomenon, we ask how the labour input per capita could have risen at 0·5 per cent a year throughout the nineteenth century as shown in the third line of Table 1. After all, there is a limit to how much a person can work, and hours

18

were not short in 1800. The answer is that people did not work longer hours in each working day, but that they worked a larger part of the year. At the beginning of the nineteenth century, most workers were agricultural workers, and agriculture is the seasonal activity *par excellence*. Farmers engaged in household manufacture and other activities in their off seasons, but these activities were neither very productive nor engaged in full time. The transfer of workers out of agriculture therefore meant that they could work more steadily throughout the year. The larger output per worker in non-agricultural activities than in agriculture noted above (in the discussion of national income before 1800) was in large part a result of the longer 'season' of non-agricultural employment.

It is true that the growth of income accounted for by this process is hardly a case of getting something for nothing. Yet the evidence indicates that agricultural workers were eager to migrate to the cities, work harder and enjoy higher incomes. Industrialisation was not limited by the reluctance of workers to forsake their farms and move to the cities. Instead, the ability of workers to get off the farm was limited by the technology existing before the Industrial Revolution. Consequently, if the rise in income per capita during the nineteenth century was not a free gift, it was still a possibility created by the growth of a new technology.

The second phenomenon visible behind the data in Table 1 concerns the growth of population noted at the beginning of this chapter. Had we been living in the eighteenth century, we would have expected that a rise in population of the magnitude described would have resulted in a massive *decrease* in living standards. Living when we do, we are not surprised at history, but we must not forget the costs of expansion that loomed so large in the minds of our ancestors. The American settlers were fortunate that the land they pushed into did not become less fertile as they moved West. The settlement of America was in this regard a different process from the one envisaged by Malthus when he discussed population growth. But the fertile lands of the American West were still far away from the sea, and some way had to be found to bring their products out. The railroad proved to be an efficient device for this job, but it was also expensive. The expansion of America was not undertaken without cost.

Looked at another way, is it not remarkable that we have had a massive capital accumulation during the nineteenth century without a corresponding fall in the rate of return on capital? It appears that the increase in the physical size of the United States was able to 'soak up' capital without running into diminishing returns. More accurately, the needs of the western expansion created a need for investment that raised the return to capital, or would have raised it if a high rate of investment had not kept the capital stock in line with the country's growing needs. Abramovitz and David [1973, *434*], the authors of Table 1, identify this process as 'capital-deepening technical change' and recognise it as another opportunity for expansion created by the Industrial Revolution.

3   The Effects of Abundant Land

HAVING established that economic growth in the United States was both rapid and sustained more or less from the founding of the Republic onwards, the historian is led naturally to inquire into the causes of this growth. It has not escaped the notice of American historians that the British Industrial Revolution was taking place at roughly the same time or slightly earlier, and that the causes of the two movements must have been closely related. Nevertheless, two characteristics of American growth have called for special explanation. First, there is the extraordinary record of growth in the total national product. For while the rate of growth of per capita income was not far from the British experience, the rate of growth of total income in the nineteenth century was almost without peer. How was it possible for the United States to absorb so many new people without retarding or even reversing this process of growth? Secondly, the British visitor to these former British colonies found economic growth taking place in a decidedly non-British social setting. What had happened to these British emigrants in their passage to the New World to make them into that rough breed of man known as Americans?

These questions are linked, because a single answer has been supplied for both : America differed from Britain because it had so much land. The tradition that emphasises the corrosive effect of abundant land upon imported social institutions is old and venerable [Diamond, 1967]. Economic historians have not differed from other historians in their acceptance of this thesis. Similarly, the idea that more land was better than less land if one was to escape Malthusian restrictions on growth has met with little opposition. Yet an increasing number of scholars have begun to question the application of this idea to American conditions. It is worth examining this heterodox literature to see if in this particular case one can argue that less land would have been preferable to more.

The total land area of the United States at different times is shown in Table 2. The large expansion in the first half of the nineteenth century was due primarily to the Louisiana Purchase in 1803. With one stroke of the diplomatic pen, the United States acquired much of its present area west of the Mississippi river and created conditions conducive to acquiring the remainder.

This land was purchased by the government of the United States, and it therefore was added to the previous stock of land owned by the government, i.e. to the public domain. The public domain was created when various states ceded to the federal government lands claimed by more than one state, mostly in the present Mid-west – the area just south of the Great Lakes. The Louisiana Purchase greatly enlarged the public domain, and various distributions from this domain, to states, railroads and individuals, decreased it. As Table 2 shows, the maximum extent

Table 2

Land Area of the United States
(Thousand million Acres)

	Total land area	*Public domain*	*Land in farms*
1802	0·5	0·2	n.a.
1850	1·9	1·2	0·3
1912	1·9	0·6	0·9
1950	1·9	0·4	1·2

Source : U.S. Bureau of Census, 1960, *236, 239.*

of the public domain was achieved around the middle of the nineteenth century when it included well over half of the land area of the United States. And, as the public domain diminished, the area of land in farms rose. Not surprisingly, the distribution of the public domain was largely a process of agricultural expansion.

There has been repeated questioning of the way in which the government chose to distribute the public domain, focusing on the role of nefarious individuals labelled 'speculators'. This term is clearly pejorative and has the additional disadvantage of lacking a precise meaning. Consequently, it is often hard to know who is being criticised or analysed. If the term is to apply to everyone who bought land with an eye toward reselling it, then surely most landowners in this peripatetic society were speculators. If it applies to individuals who bought large amounts of land, then we must presume that any profits earned from owning the land reflected a diversity of motivations and actions. In fact, most investigators have restricted their empirical work to people who both bought large tracts of land and also sold it relatively quickly, and we may adopt that use of the term here.

The question is whether the speculators earned an unreasonable profit from their activities, i.e. if they used the land-distribution system of the government in some way to deprive the settlers of their rightful return from the land. It must be admitted at the outset that these speculators were entitled to some profits. They acted as brokers – buying large parcels of land, subdividing them and selling small lots to individual settlers – and they were entitled to a competitive rate of return for these activities. The government was happy to sell to speculators because it was reluctant to act as its own broker. Preferring to be a wholesaler rather than a retailer, the government acquiesced in a system in which profit was to be made by purchasing and reselling land.

The question then is whether the profits that speculators earned were in some sense excessive, i.e. above a competitive rate of return. Unless these profits – should they be found – are to be attributed to luck or to the special circumstances of some speculators, any unusual profits must have been the results of market power on the part of the speculators. But how could these people acquire monopoly power? If the government had acted as the monopolist it was, then it would have charged the profit-maximising price for the land and there would not have been any profit left over for the speculators.

The use of auctions to sell land can be interpreted as an attempt to extract monopoly profits from the sale of land. Since the price of each parcel of land could differ, the government appears to have been trying to be the most profitable sort of monopolist, a discriminating monopolist who charged each individual the maximum price that he was willing to pay.

Before concluding that there was no room left for private profit, we must remember that land auctions were held periodically as the country was surveyed and that land was not auctioned more than once. The land not sold at auction was then offered for sale by the government at a legislatively-set minimum price. The average price paid for land was not far from this minimum; if the government wanted to be a discriminating monopolist, its desire apparently outran its ability.

We therefore cannot rule out the possibility that monopoly profit was to be gained by private speculators. How large an opportunity this represented has not been ascertained, and the mechanism by which it could have been exploited is also unclear. It is no less true of individuals than of governments that they must have market power to make monopoly profits. How did private individuals acquire monopoly rights over public property offered for sale to all? Investigators typically have approached these questions only tangentially, preferring to ask if there were any profits before examining the process by which they could have been acquired. Unfortunately, the empirical data have not clarified the issue. Bogue and Bogue [1957] revealed, in a classic article and review of the literature, that speculators' profits had not been higher than a brokerage commission might have been expected to have been. But Swierenga [1966], on the basis of a new sample and different methodology, argues that speculators earned profits of up to 50 per cent on invested capital. No honest broker ever made profits like these. Both the theory and history await further clarification.

An entirely separate question about the distribution of benefits from new land concerns the effect of increased cotton production on its price. Wright [1971] estimated an econometric model of the *ante bellum* (pre-Civil War) cotton market. In this model the demand for British cotton textiles is shown to have been either inelastic or not very elastic, depending on which of several estimates you prefer. The derived demand for American raw cotton therefore was inelastic also. (Here, as elsewhere, I am condensing in Procrustean fashion a longer discussion.) It follows that if all other things were held constant, then an expansion of cotton production on the basis of new land would have lowered the price received by cotton growers as a group enough to reduce their

24

total revenues. This is not to assert that individual cotton growers were being impoverished in the *ante bellum* period, since many, many things were changing at the same time that cotton production was growing. It is rather to say that the influence of territorial expansion considered in isolation was to make total revenues from growing cotton lower than they would have been in the absence of this expansion.

This argument has two corollaries. First, a more rapid distribution of land would have decreased the income of cotton growers [Passell, 1971]. It therefore would have been rational for Southerners to have opposed the distribution of Western cotton lands, even if these lands were to have been given to existing landowners free. Secondly, it would have been in the interests of slave owners to have done likewise. More land would have increased the ratio of land to labour in growing cotton, since the size of the slave labour force was not affected by land policy, and this would have increased the marginal physical product of labour. But it would have also decreased the price of cotton, and the value of the marginal product of slave labour would not have risen. The effect on slave prices of faster land distribution therefore would have been adverse [Passell and Wright, 1972]. A slave-owning cotton grower therefore should have opposed rapid land distribution both because revenues from growing cotton would have gone down and the value of his slave capital would have followed suit.

The reasoning used to reach these conclusions is far too complex to detail here, but their dependence on the existence of an inelastic demand curve for cotton must be emphasised. If accepted, the argument has implications that are of the greatest interest. (The implications for *British* economic history of an inelastic demand curve for cotton textiles are numerous also, but not of concern here.) It is clear that the introduction of new cotton lands increased the production of cotton and aggregate real income. The argument just given asserts that not everyone shared in the rise in income. Cotton growers as a class suffered relative to what they would have earned if the new lands had been left untouched. The slave-owning portion of this class suffered additionally through the impact of the value of their slaves. (It is hard

25

to say if the slaves also lost out without knowing how closely slave consumption and slave productivity were tied.)

Someone must have gained, since more cotton is better than less; who was it? If it was not the growers of cotton, it must have been either the people who made raw cotton into textiles or the people who consumed these textiles. Further work is needed to know which group gained most, but one tentative conclusion stands out even without this determination. Most cotton grown in America was made into yarn and cloth in Britain and consumed outside America. The benefits of the distribution of American cotton lands therefore were enjoyed largely outside the United States, and chiefly in Britain.

Not all new land was used for growing cotton, and the effect of new lands on the production of wheat has also been studied. The focus here has been on the late nineteenth century, due to the paucity of *ante bellum* data on the production of wheat. Two approaches have been taken, neither the same as the approach used for cotton.

In the first such approach, Parker and Klein [1966] attempted to discover the effect of the westward expansion on the productivity of labour used to grow wheat (and other small grains). Using a procedure reminiscent of the one used by David in his extrapolation of national income data, they decomposed the change in labour productivity into the sum of the change within each region (due largely to mechanisation) and the change resulting from shifting the labour force from the East to the West. Less than one-fifth of the change in labour productivity could be explained by the shifting location of labour. Parker and Klein concluded that mechanisation, not the westward expansion, was the driving force behind the increase in wheat-growing labour productivity in the second half of the nineteenth century.

The assumptions used in this calculation need to be understood if its significance is to be evaluated correctly. Parker and Klein talk only of productivity, that is, output per man. They do not discuss the enormous increase in the total production of wheat over this half-century. Implicitly, they appear to be saying that the productivity of labour in the cultivation of wheat would have been substantially the same as it was in 1900 even if there had been no westward expansion. But at what scale would wheat have been grown in the United States if the West had not been won?

The demand for wheat, both in the United States and abroad, grew rapidly in the late nineteenth century. If the western lands had not been used, the demand would have been intensified at other locations. (I assume that population growth would not have been affected by the closure of the West; modification of this assumption can give still further results.) The supply of wheat from a given acre is not infinitely elastic, and the increased demand would have met an upward-sloping supply curve. The price of wheat would have risen and land would have been cultivated more intensively. Labour productivity would have fallen. Parker and Klein's calculation therefore is incomplete because it does not take into consideration the change in demand that accompanied the westward expansion.

In an alternative approach to this question, Fisher and Temin [1970] asked whether the demand in 1900 could have been satisfied from the eastern states alone. Their argument involved the estimation of supply curves for wheat on a state-by-state basis. They found that the elasticity of supply of wheat was near one, and that it would have been very difficult to produce the actual 1900 wheat production from the eastern states alone. If the West had not been opened, it follows that the price of wheat would have been higher and the production lower than they actually were in 1900. The United States probably would have lacked one of its primary sources of foreign exchange, and the European agricultural depression could have been less pronounced. (Population patterns might also have been different.) If the West had remained wild, labour productivity in American agriculture probably would have been lower, but that undoubtedly is one of the smallest differences between this hypothetical world and the actual one. As with cotton, the effects of American geographical expansion spread beyond the political boundaries of the United States.

The effects of abundant land in the United States extended beyond the agricultural sector also. A traditional argument asserts that the availability of land in the United States increased labour productivity in American industry. This argument was articulated in the nineteenth century and extended recently by Habakkuk [1962]. In his complex analysis he discussed the availability of land, the skill-distribution of labour, the elasticity of the supply of labour, the characteristics of demand, technical change and other topics. For the sake of concreteness, the discussion here will be confined to the simplest aspect of this argument and even to a single proposition. This proposition asserts that the abundance of American land raised the American wage rate and forced American manufacturers to use more capital per worker. In other words, the high ratio of land to labour in American agriculture led in turn to a high ratio of capital to labour in American manufacturing.

In what circumstances will this proposition be true? We will not try to enumerate all of them, but rather to find a model in the spirit of the literature in which it will be true. The model recognises only three distinct factors of production – land, labour, capital – for a start. Two additional assumptions serve to produce the desired proposition. First, assume that land is used only in agriculture and that capital is used only in manufacturing. Secondly, assume that the relative price of agricultural and manufactured goods is fixed (because they are traded internationally at fixed prices). In these circumstances an expansion of land will increase the demand for labour in agriculture, drain labour away from manufacturing into agriculture, and raise the capital–labour ratio in manufacturing as a result [Temin, 1966*b*, 1971].

These assumptions produce the desired proposition, but they also produce some unwanted propositions as well. In particular, since the capital–labour ratio in manufacturing is raised by the abundance of land and there are only two factors of production (labour and capital) in manufacturing, the rate of return to capital should have been decreased. If this model is to be used to explain why American labour productivity was higher than British in the nineteenth century, it must rest not only on the observation of abundant land in America but also on the low productivity of capital in America. Our indexes of capital productivity are crude at best, but the best available proxy, the interest rate, was *higher* in the United States than in Britain.

This apparent paradox has led to widespread disaffection with the simple model just outlined. Modifications have been suggested in which the original proposition remains true. But since some analogue of the unwelcome corollary generally has remained true also in the modified models, they have not been well received. Dissatisfaction with these models has led the discussion to shift away from the question of explaining labour scarcity in American manufacturing – a phenomenon 'known' only from inference from simple models like the one just outlined and not actually observed – to the question of finding a suitable model to assess the impact of American land on American manufacturing.

One such model does away with the first assumption of this simple model. If land is used in both sectors, then one cannot say which sector will lose labour as a result of abundant land. If one says that land is used in manufacturing only indirectly – that is, that land itself is not used in manufacturing but agricultural output is – then the effects are more complex [Fogel, 1967]. Under reasonable production conditions, labour will be drawn out of manufacturing into agriculture, but the availability of more agricultural goods will raise the productivity of the remaining factors of production in manufacturing. This model has not been worked out, and it is not clear if it resolves the paradox at hand; it does, however, provide a lead into a richer way to model this process.

An alternative approach has been to keep the first assumption but reject the second [Passell and Schmundt, 1971]. It is then possible to produce effects similar to those discussed above with reference to the cotton market. The new land will make agricultural goods more plentiful. If the demand for agricultural goods is sufficiently inelastic, this may lower the price enough to reduce the demand for labour in agriculture. In that case, more land would mean more labour in manufacturing, more manufacturing production and higher productivity of capital in manufacturing. We do not know that this is a more realistic model than the others; the choice of a 'good' model is still a question for future research.

Let us return to our starting point. Do we wish to oppose the long-standing view that more land was better than less? The answer must surely be 'no', although we can now say that not everyone affected by the settlement of the West would have been willing to agree. The availability of land in the United States encouraged economic growth both in the United States and elsewhere, but the benefits of this growth were not spread evenly among the population. At any moment of time, there probably were people whose interests would have been served by a restriction on western settlement. We do not know how many such people there were, for even an uneven distribution of benefits may bring some benefits to everyone. But we are well advised to be sensitive to the distribution of benefits of the complex and intricate process called economic growth.

In particular, the expansion of western agriculture shown in Table 2 affected both agriculture and industry in the East. The output from western agriculture competed with the output from eastern agriculture. While the consumer benefited from the resulting lower prices, the eastern farmer apparently did not. Western farms competed with industry in the labour market, rather than the product market, and the presumption has been that this competition impeded the growth of American industry. This presumption has been shown to be excessively simple, but recent work has succeeded only in questioning the traditional idea, not in refuting it.

4 Technological Change

AS we have seen, there are a variety of theories linking American economic growth to the abundance of American land. But there are also other theories about American economic growth, many of which centre on what economists call technological change. This phrase refers to changes in the ways of doing things – manufacturing goods, transporting goods and people, providing services to consumers. There are many different kinds of technological change and many different theories that deal with it.

One theory follows the lines of the work summarised in Table 1 (page 17 above). Assume that in the absence of technological change a doubling of the economy's inputs will double the economy's output. Then we can start from some point in history and compare the growth rates of the economy's inputs and output. The difference between these growth rates is then defined to be the rate of technological change. However, as Abramovitz and David [1973] have shown, this is a theory that is more interesting when applied to the twentieth century than to the nineteenth, because the rate of technological change defined in this way was not very rapid in the nineteenth century.

A separate group of theories revolves around the observation that the composition of the economy's output and of its capital stock has changed dramatically over the past two hundred years. Technological change, from this vantage point, consists in the introduction of new machines and products. The theories concern particular industries and activities rather than the economy as a whole. The concept of technological change is considerably less abstract.

There is no conflict between these theories, because the absence of technical change that affects the relation between all inputs taken together and aggregate output, does not mean that the composition of inputs and outputs has not changed. And it is obvious from simple observation that we do not make things the way we used to and that the relationship between men and machines has been subject to a great deal of change.

Changes were most apparent in the early nineteenth century in the areas of cotton textiles, power generation, and metallurgy. The British innovations in spinning and weaving were adopted in America and transformed to suit American conditions. The steam engine came into use in America with the invention of the high-pressure engine, and Americans mostly used this engine rather than the Watt engine still being used in Britain. The iron industry was revolutionised by changes in the manufacture of both pig iron and wrought iron. In the former, coal was adopted as fuel; in the latter, rolling mills replaced forges.

As the nineteenth century wore on, these areas were joined by others in which both the methods used and the products produced changed. And a distinctive American style in manufacturing methods began to appear. Manufacturers in America, starting with the makers of small arms and similar items like clocks and locks, made their products of interchangeable parts.

The parts of a musket or clock were not specific to that musket or clock; if a part was broken or mislaid, it could be replaced by another without extensive alterations to make the new piece fit. This procedure therefore eliminated the costly fitting expenses inherent in the older handicraft production [Rosenberg, 1972, chapter 4].

The theories – for there are many of them – that relate how these changes came about and how this style emerged are varied indeed. Economic historians have been exceedingly curious about the specific changes that individual industries and productive processes have undergone. Consequently there are detailed studies of the introduction of the power loom in the early nineteenth century [Zevin, 1971] and the Draper loom in the late nineteenth century [Feller, 1966]; of improvements in ocean shipping in the eighteenth century [Walton, 1968] and in railroads in the nineteenth [Fishlow, 1966]; of the introduction of steam engines [Temin, 1966a], of power in general [Fenichel, 1966], and of coal in blast furnaces [Temin, 1964, chapter 3].

Rather than survey the conclusions of these studies, it seems more useful to inquire into the argument of one of them to see its nature. I have selected one by David [1966] on the introduction of the reaper, both because it is unusually explicit about its theoretical structure and because it typifies the kind of reasoning used in these studies. The arguments of other studies can be scrutinised similarly, leading sometimes to a confirmation of the author's conclusions and sometimes not.

David set himself to explain the *timing* of the adoption of the mechanical horse-drawn reaper in the American Mid-west. The reaper had been introduced in the 1830s, but it was not widely adopted until the 1850s. While there were improvements in the machine, they were concentrated largely in the early years of its production, and the period when the reaper was being adopted widely was not a period of rapid change in the reaper itself. Why, then, was the reaper adopted widely in the 1850s?

There are two traditional theories. Both start from the observation that wheat prices rose in the 1850s, partly as a result of the Crimean War. One theory asserts that this price rise led to an expansion of wheat production which required an increase in the inputs to wheat production. These inputs were primarily land and labour. But while land was in elastic supply so that more land could be used without markedly raising its price, labour was in relatively inelastic supply. The increased demand for labour therefore raised wage rates and made the use of machines to harvest the crop more attractive. A second theory asserts that the rise in the price of wheat led individual farmers to expand the size of their farms. Because there was a limit to the amount of grain that a man could cut with hand tools (scythe and cradle), farmers changed to reapers as their farms got bigger. Or to state this theory differently but equivalently, while the cost of harvesting by hand was less than the cost of harvesting by machine for a small farm, it was more expensive for a larger farm.

David synthesises these theories by employing the diagram shown in Figure 1. The curve marked AC_H shows the average cost – that is, the cost per acre – of harvesting wheat from any number of acres by hand. The curve marked AC_M shows the average cost of harvesting by means of machine, that is, with a horse-drawn

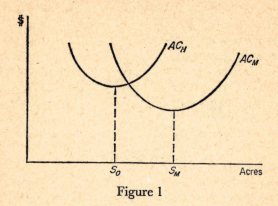

Figure 1

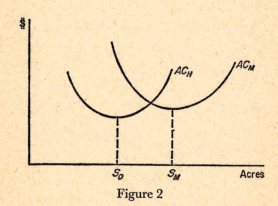

Figure 2

34

reaper. At the optimum-size farm using hand methods, S_O, the machine method was more expensive than the hand method. At the optimum size farm using the reaper, S_M, however, the cost of harvesting by reaper was not only lower than the cost of harvesting by hand at that size but also at any other size also. In other words, if the farmer was free to choose the number of acres on which he planted wheat, he would minimise his costs by planting S^M acres and using a reaper.

Why did the farmers not do this? According to David, the average size of farms was considerably smaller than S_M, and it was expensive to expand. In his words: 'The costs of acquiring, clearing, and fencing new land, or simply of preparing land already held, were hardly insignificant even on the open prairies' [David, 1966, *19*]. This is not a precise statement, and it fails to discriminate between two hypotheses. First, these costs may have been prohibitive under the conditions and institutions of the 1850s. Or, secondly, the costs may have been present but within reach of farmers, whether by borrowing, co-operating with their neighbours, or other means. Given all that we know about American farming in the 1850s, it is hard to accept the first possibility. To give just one suggestive fact, let us remember that the crops for which the reaper could be used (wheat, oats and rye) were not the only crops grown in the Mid-west at this time. In particular, much of the land was used to grow corn (maize), for which the reaper was not suitable. Farmers could have expanded their wheat acreage by switching out of maize into wheat. In fact, given economies of scale as shown in Figure 1, farmers should have done just this, and we should find that farms were specialised in either small grain production or in maize.

If we accept the second hypothesis, then we have to ask again why farmers did not plant S_M acres in wheat (and oats and rye). The obvious answer is that the costs of expansion made the minimum cost of the machine process more expensive than the minimum cost of the hand process. The cost per acre of expansion should be entered in Figure 1 as part of the costs of the machine process. In addition to the costs used by David to derive Figure 1, we must include the carrying cost of the land used.

(These costs would be interest costs if the farmer borrowed to pay for the expenses cited by David, but they could also be *opportunity costs* if the farmer switched land from other uses to use for wheat.) These costs will be proportional to the acreage used, and they will raise the AC_M curve relative to the AC_H curve. We may assume for the purposes of the argument that they raised it far enough to make the minimum point of the AC_M curve higher than the minimum point of the AC_H curve as shown in Figure 2. Farmers then were maximising profits at the start of the 1850s by producing at S_O.

As the wage rate rose in the 1850s, the costs for hand reaping rose relative to the costs for machine reaping. Let us suppose that they rose enough to transform the cost structure shown in Figure 2 into the cost structure shown in Figure 1, where the costs now include the costs of the acreage used. Then the changes in costs would have led farmers to expand wheat production from S_O acres to S_M acres. The observed expansion of wheat acreage, in other words, would have been the result of the adoption of the reaper, not the cause. The cause was the rise in the wage rate.

This discussion suggests that David's emphasis on the size of farms was misplaced, but that his conclusions should properly be stated even more strongly than they were. He concluded that the major explanatory variable was the wage rate, but that increasing farm size aided the adoption of the reaper. We can now say that the rise in the wage rate produced both the increased adoption of the reaper and the expanded farm size. (The argument, even the amended argument given here, assumes that reapers could not be used in common by several farmers or rented for short periods of time. If they could have been, then the importance of farm size is even further reduced.)

Several observations can be made about this discussion. First, the model used to explain the adoption of a new machine assumed that the potential users of the machine (farmers in this case) were rational profit maximisers. Second, it was assumed that prices were the result of supplies and demands (so that the wage rate varied with the demand for labour). Third, the model – though impressive in its architecture – is not the only model that can be used to explain this historical event. And fourth, the conclusions emerge strengthened, albeit with a little different emphasis, by a modification of the model. The first three of these points are typical of the literature on specific innovations. The last point is only sometimes true, and the literature needs to be handled with care.

5   *Railroads*

ONE innovation above all has been singled out as having a critical role in American economic development, and a considerable literature has grown up about it. I refer of course to the railroad. Many historians have contented themselves with descriptions and analyses of the railroads themselves and left the question of their impact on the rest of the economy relatively open. The past decade, however, has seen a change in this approach, focusing on the use of the concept of 'social savings'.

At the start of the nineteenth century, waterborne transportation was far cheaper than overland transport. Goods travelling within the United States moved along the Atlantic coast and down the Mississippi river and its tributaries. (Only a few goods moved up the river for obvious reasons.) The changes in the costs of transportation in the first third of the nineteenth century encouraged the use of water routes. Steam was applied to existing water routes, making it economically feasible to ship a larger variety of goods up rivers as well as down, and the number of water routes within the United States was increased by digging canals. The Erie canal, which connected the Great Lakes and the Atlantic seaboard, was both the most important and the most successful of these canals. In retrospect, it may have been the only one to have a significant effect on American economic growth [Goodrich, 1960].

The introduction of the railroad around 1830 decisively changed the relationship between water and land transportation. By 1840, there were as many miles of railroads in the United States as canals (see Table 3). By 1850, there were over twice as many miles of railroads as canals. And almost no new canals were dug after then. The switch from water to land transportation changed the appearance of the United States; the question before us is whether it had other effects as well.

Table 3

Mileage of Canals and Railroads
(Thousands of miles)

	Canals	Railroads
1830	1·3	a
1840	3·3	3·3
1850	3·7	8·9
1860	b	30·6
1870	b	52·9
1880	b	93·3
1890	b	166·7

Notes : *a* : less than 0·5.

      b : not available; not appreciably larger than the 1850 figure.

Source : Taylor [1951, *79*]; U.S. Bureau of the Census [1960, *427*].

'Social savings' were introduced into the discussion of American railroads by Fogel [1962]. They are defined as the difference between the actual national product and the national product that would have been produced without the railroads. They are measured by the difference in the cost of shipping the goods that actually travelled by railroad between the railroad and the next best alternative. This cost difference in turn is measured by multiplying the unit price differential between the railroad and its alternative by the quantity of goods transported by railroad.

Social savings were first calculated by Fogel [1960, 1962, 1964] for American railroads in 1890. He was followed almost immediately by Fishlow [1965], who used data from 1859. These two authors have been followed by others investigating both railroads and canals [Boyd and Walton, 1972; Ransom, 1964, 1970], and the concept has recently been applied to English railroads also [Hawke, 1970].

Now it is far from obvious that this simple product can be equated to a change in the national product, and we must ask how this particular measure of social savings is justified. There are at least three implicit assumptions in the argument. First, the ob-

39

served prices must be good indexes of (social) costs. Secondly, the costs must remain constant over the range affected by the shift of traffic. And thirdly, these costs must be the only costs to society of the absence of railroads. We examine these propositions in turn.

1. A problem arises immediately with the first step. Railroads and alternative means of transportation offer similar but not identical services. If one uses simply the quoted prices per ton-mile of different transportation systems, a part of the cost to society is being ignored. Specifically, if railroads offered better service than their competitors, part of the cost to society of doing without the railroads would be in a deterioration of transportation services. It is necessary therefore to adjust the prices of the alternative transportation systems to make them reflect an equivalent level of service to the railroads [Fogel, 1964; Fishlow, 1965].

Even after this is done, an uneasiness about the equation of price to cost remains. Economic theory tells us that prices will equal marginal costs in a competitive industry, but were the railroads (or their alternatives) competitive? It is hard to read the protests against railroad monopoly in the second half of the nineteenth century without wondering if some of them were justified. And it is hard to rationalise the formation of the Interstate Commerce Commission in 1887 to regulate railroad rates if the railroads were in a competitive industry. The suggestion – partly confirmed by direct cost measurements – that prices were not equal to marginal costs must be allowed [Lebergott, 1966].

2. The second step in the argument is equally hard. The observed price differential of the alternative transportation systems measures the cost to the shipper (assumed now to be equal to the cost to society) of switching goods between these systems at the actual level of use. When we talk about doing without the railroad in 1890, however, we are talking about switching the bulk of transported goods from one transportation system to another. Can we be sure that the unit costs of making this switch will not be affected by this large movement? Phrased in another way, could the alternative means of transport carry all the goods that actually went by railroad without an increase in costs? If water transport is used, the capacity of locks has to be considered

[McClelland, 1968]. If horses and wagons are used, the problems of stabling and feeding them have to be solved [David, 1969]. Just as it was not obvious that all the wheat that was actually produced could have been produced at a reasonable cost in the absence of the westward movement, it is not obvious that all the goods that were transported by railroad could have been transported by other facilities at a reasonable cost.

3. The third step is by far the hardest. It assumes that in the absence of railroads, everything else in the economy would have gone on as if there were railroads. People would have produced the same goods, transported the same goods and consumed the same goods (less the increased cost of transportation). They would have acted as if they were responding to one set of prices (those with the railroad) when they were in fact faced with another set (those without railroads). It is hard to rationalise such odd behaviour. Fogel [1964] tried to amend his measure of social savings to take account of possible changes in people's behaviour. Our theory tells us that costs are always as high or higher when constraints are present than when they are not. Consequently, removing the constraint that people must not change their behaviour when the railroads vanish cannot make people worse off. And it is reasonable to suppose that they would have been better off to adjust their behaviour to the prices they faced than to continue patterns prompted by another price structure. Farmers on the prairie, for example, would not have shipped their products to market by wagon and canal if the profits from doing so were negative. They would have moved to the city instead and been better off. Allowing people to adjust to the absence of railroads therefore reduces the social savings.

But the adjustment allowed by Fogel is only partial. It is as if the railroads were constructed and then abandoned. For all of the capital equipment actually built and all the technical changes actually made are presumed to exist in the world without railroads just as they did in the actual world. One can visualise two hypothetical worlds. In one of them the railroads were built and then abandoned. In the other, railroads were never introduced at all. Authors who calculate social savings appear to be discussing the first of these worlds, but they often talk as if they are discussing the second. Yet it is highly probable that the two hypothetical worlds are different, and very hard to say in which one the national product was higher [David, 1969].

Each of these three implicit assumptions has been questioned, leading at least one investigator to cry 'Halt!' to the proceedings [McClelland, 1972]. A suspicion may be entertained, however, that the problem is not really in the estimation. True, there are problems with the numbers brought forth by Fogel, Fishlow and others. But there are always questions that can be raised about quantitative work. And a dispute that has occupied the attention of so many people seldom revolves simply around numbers. There are many questions that could be asked about the impact of railroads on American economic history, and social savings illuminate only a few of them. Much of the criticism of this concept can be interpreted as a call for a redefinition of the question rather than a recomputation of the numbers.

An alternative question concerns the construction of the railroads. Even if the services of the railroads had been only infinitesimally better than the alternatives, were there benefits (or disadvantages) from the construction and operation of the railroad that would not have come from the alternative means? The main difference between railroads and the alternatives from this point of view was that railroads used the outputs of industries thought to be central to the process of economic growth, i.e. iron, steel and machinery. Fogel [1964] examined the link to the iron and steel industry and concluded it was not important. The railroads used large quantities of rails before the Civil War, but rails were largely imported. The effect of the railroad demand on American blast furnaces consequently was small. This conclusion ignores the effect of railroads on American rolling mills which were heavily involved in the production of rails and which were the vehicle through which the Bessemer process was introduced into America after the Civil War. But while railroads used most of the Bessemer steel produced before about 1880 and may be presumed to have been instrumental in the adoption of the Bessemer process, Fogel [1966] argued that the Bessemer process was used almost exclusively to make rails and that the benefit to the economy of using this process was better railroads and little else. The benefits of

42

the Bessemer process, then, are included in the social savings calculation; they are not in addition. The evidence for this conclusion is that the production of Bessemer steel in America fell off sharply when the demand for rails fell at the end of the nineteenth century. Most of the steel used outside the railroads in America was made by the open-hearth process.

The implicit assumption in this argument is that the introduction of the open-hearth process was independent of the introduction and exploitation of the Bessemer process. Technical arguments can be adduced to show how different the two processes are, but technical characteristics are not the only determinants of invention. Perhaps the use of the Bessemer process encouraged more research into alternative ways of making steel by demonstrating the extent of the demand for steel. Or perhaps its very success discouraged research that might have produced the open-hearth process sooner. Questions like this are hard, but they enter into any discussion of the causation of technical change.

Another characteristic of railroad construction is its expense. Between 10 and 20 per cent of gross domestic investment was allocated to the railroads between 1850 and 1880 [Gallman, 1966]. The phenomenal expense of the railroads was one of the main components of the capital deepening shown in the aggregate data. If the railroad had not existed, these investment funds could have been used elsewhere in the economy. If the alternative transportation systems that would have been used were more capital-intensive than the railroads, then all of these resources and more would have been needed there. But it is at least possible that alternative transportation systems were less capital-intensive than the railroad. In that case, resources could have gone into other industries, where their benefits might have offset the greater transportation cost stemming from the absence of railroads. An optimal development plan for the United States, in other words, might not have included the railroad!

The introduction of investment into this discussion is very important, because it changes a purely static argument into a dynamic one. The words of many articles have focused on questions of economic growth, but the calculations have usually been directed to a particular point of time. The question of the relationship between what happens at a particular moment and the whole growth process needs to be articulated. For example, if a neo-classical growth model underlies the discussion, then only the rate of population growth and the rate of technological change affect the rate of growth in the long run [Solow, 1970]. Changes in other variables may affect the level of growth or may lead to a temporary deviation from the equilibrium growth path, but they have no effect on the equilibrium growth rate. Discussions based on this model will find little long-run effect from any specific event, whether it be the construction of railroads or a major war. Consequently, fruitful research on the dynamic effects of different events will have to either focus on the short run (a few decades or less) or rely on different growth models.

The introduction of investment costs also reminds us that we typically do not discuss benefits without costs. It is one thing to say that social savings (or some other measurement of benefits) were large or small; it is quite another to say that they represented a good or bad return to the capital invested. To answer this question it is necessary to calculate a (social) rate of return for railroads and compare it with other possibilities.

There is no conceptual problem in the estimation of the capital on which to calculate such a rate, although there are many problems of measurement. The benefits resulting from this capital stock, however, include all of the things we have been discussing thus far. Instead of reopening the question of benefits, most investigators have simply used railroad earnings plus the social saving as a measure of the railroads' social benefits [Fishlow, 1965; Nerlove, 1966; David, 1969]. This has many obvious problems, some of which should be apparent from the discussion of social savings. The rates of return derived in this fashion range from 15 to about 25 per cent, which appear to be high enough to justify the existence of the railroad network in the face of alternative investments.

The discussion thus far has been conducted on the premise that the choice was between the existing railroad network and no railroads at all. But this is an extreme choice. An alternative question would be to ask if more or less railroads would have been desirable. And light can be shed on this question by asking if

44

the marginal social profitability of railroads was greater or less than the alternatives. If it was greater, then there is a prima facie case for the construction of more railroads; if it was smaller, it supports the contention that railroads were overbuilt. The marginal rate of return can be calculated by an extension of the method alluded to just above, and the estimates derived from Fogel's and Fishlow's data both imply that the marginal social rate of return from railroads was about 15 per cent. This is a respectable rate, but it is not out of line with other marginal rates of return in the economy. We may suggest, therefore, that the railroad network was a reasonable investment for the American economy, carried out at reasonable levels.

Historians who saw the railroads as the centrepiece of economic growth and historians who saw them as irrelevant to growth overstated their cases. The railroad was an important component of investment in the nineteenth century, and it yielded a social rate of return high enough to justify this expenditure, despite the financial disasters that overtook many railroads in the 1890s. It had effects on the economy that were perhaps less spectacular than contemporary observers thought, but which were still not negligible. The history of the American economy cannot be written without substantial attention to the railroads.

6 Banking

THE American banking system has been studied primarily as a source of instability in the American economy. This can be seen as an aspect of the relationship between banks and economic growth, since depressions are an interruption to growth. This connection, however, is a bit forced, and we shall confront directly the relationship between banks and growth. The discussion will be preceded by a description of the American banking system and followed by some comments on nineteenth-century depressions.

The framers of the Constitution dealt with the troublesome question of paper money by ignoring it; the Republic would have a metallic currency, and the government was empowered to take appropriate actions to introduce and regulate it. Alexander Hamilton, the first Secretary of the Treasury, therefore had considerable leeway in his dealings with banks. He proposed that the national government charter a bank for twenty years and that all paper money redeemable in specie (i.e. coin) on demand should be accepted by the federal government as if it were actually coin. The Bank of the United States was established in 1791, and its charter was allowed to expire at the end of twenty years. A new bank by the same name was chartered in 1816, again for twenty years. A bill to recharter this bank was vetoed by President Andrew Jackson in 1832 as part of the famous Bank War, and its charter expired in 1836. The government continued to receive bank notes redeemable in specie throughout the rise and fall of these banks, discontinuing this practice only with the creation of the Independent Treasury in 1846.

The actions of the federal government therefore allowed the states to charter banks more or less at will. The states entered into this activity with great enthusiasm; there were almost one thousand banks in 1840 and over 1500 in 1860. These banks issued notes (i.e. promises by the bank to pay specie on demand) and cheques (requests by individuals to the bank to pay notes or specie on the demand of another individual). Contemporary discussions are expressed in terms of notes, and historians assumed that cheques were introduced late in the *ante bellum* period. Nevertheless, cheques were used from the start of the nineteenth century, spreading from the urban areas throughout the country [Van Fenstermaker, 1965].

The state banks generally were responsive to requests for specie payments, but the system was not free of problems. Since banks were located all over the country, a note of a distant bank (or a cheque drawn on a distant bank) was not worth as much as a note (or cheque) from a local bank. There was typically uncertainty about the reliability of the faraway bank. And even if a person knew that the distant bank was a responsible one, there were costs of sending the note to the bank and retrieving the specie.

The conditions that gave rise to this uncertainty and these costs also created opportunities for fraud, and the abuses of the state banking system are well known. They ranged from the establishment of the 'wildcat banks' (located so far into the woods that even a wildcat could not reach them to redeem its notes) to outright counterfeiting. One way to see the legislative history of the *ante bellum* years as it pertains to banks is as a continuing effort to reduce the opportunity for fraud and the uncertainty surrounding notes of distant banks [Hammond, 1957]. Despite the volume of legislation and commentary, however, it is doubtful that the costs to society of this loose system were very great. One may hazard the guess, for example, that the costs were no more than those associated with the use today of credit cards, where the opportunities for fraud also are large.

A quite separate problem was created by the periodic refusal of banks to redeem their notes and cash cheques in specie at par. During the banking panics of the early nineteenth century, American banks 'suspended payments'. They did not completely refuse to pay out specie; they simply refused to pay one dollar of specie for a dollar bill. In other words, they stopped maintaining the specie price of their obligations (notes and desposits) at par. They did not go out of business; they did not even refuse entirely to deal in specie. They were acting against the law, since the obligation to redeem notes was a contractual obligation. But when all banks at once refused to honour their obligations, the legal remedies were ineffective.

These bank suspensions had several effects. They created a two-tier system of currency, with a floating exchange rate between them. Paper currency was used for local transactions, but paper money depreciated rapidly with distance from the issuing bank since its value was based solely on the bank's good name and it could *not* be used to pay taxes – the best way of 'redeeming' notes when banks were paying out specie at par. International transactions were conducted in terms of specie, and since the price of paper currency fell relative to specie, the introduction of floating exchange rates between them led to devaluation by the United States relative to Britain and other countries. International trade therefore was affected by bank suspensions.

The system of state banks ran into severe trouble during the Civil War. The federal government responded by issuing its own currency, the famous Greenbacks, and by establishing the National Banking System [Sharkey, 1959; Hammond, 1970]. State bank-notes backed by specie were replaced by national bank-notes backed by bonds of the federal government [Friedman and Schwartz, 1963; Cagan, 1965]. State banks – although not state bank-notes – and bank panics continued to exist, and the Federal Reserve System was superimposed upon the National Banking System in 1914 in an effort to eliminate the panics.

With this introduction, let us turn to the connection between banks and economic growth. Banks are financial intermediaries. They borrow in one market and lend in others, thereby providing communication between different parts of the economy and paths through which available resources in the hands of one group can be placed at the disposal of another group (for a price). We inquire first into the uses of these resources and then into their sources.

The largest use of bank financing was in international and inter-regional trade. It took a long time, often several months, for goods to go from seller to buyer under the transportation technology of

48

the nineteenth century. Who was to own the goods in the meantime? The problem was solved in America, as in Britain, by use of bills of exchange : a negotiable instrument that allowed a third party to finance the transfer of goods. A seller drew a bill of exchange on a buyer who then 'accepted' it by signing it. The accepted bill then was a promissory note from the buyer obliging him to pay a specified sum of money at a specified time and place. It could be sold, but since it was not worth as much at the time and place of sale as it would be at the time and place of its redemption by the buyer, it was sold at a discount. (The process was therefore called discounting, and the accepted bills were referred to either as acceptances or as discounts.) Banks were very active in the market for these bills.

A second use of bank financing was for industrial enterprises, and there can be no doubt that the pattern observed in Britain was reproduced to some extent in the United States; many industrial activities were financed out of the web of commercial credit just described [Pollard, 1964]. All firms operated with large volumes of financial obligations and credits, and an increase in the former relative to the latter was an increase in the capital available to the firm. In addition, railroads and New England textile firms issued stocks and bonds that were held at times by banks.

Where did the resources come from that were utilised by American merchants and producers? The credit extended through bills of exchange was extended by the person who held the bill during the time between its acceptance and its redemption. It is hard to know with any certainty who these people were, but the available evidence suggests strongly that many U.S. bills were held in Britain. Enough of the bills were held there to make a change in the terms under which people in Britain were willing to hold them (such as the change that took place when the Bank of England refused to discount them in 1836), a critical event for the short-term health of the American economy [Matthews, 1954; Temin, 1969].

The ownership of railroad and industrial stocks and bonds is known even less well, except in the case of the New England textile firms studied by Davis [1958]. These firms had bank loans, but they were small relative to their total assets. The largest single group of stockholders was the merchants, who held between one-fifth and two-fifths of the stock outstanding by major textile firms before the Civil War. Professional persons were the second largest category, followed by a large number of smaller and diverse groups. It appears that these firms were able to draw capital from the Boston area largely without the agency of banks.

The proportion of total American investment that was financed through the banking system was quite small. The New England textile firms did not rely primarily on banks, nor did the railroads. Farm improvement, which was a large proportion of investment in America, particularly in the early nineteenth century, was financed partly by reduced consumption on the part of the farmer and partly by mortgages. Some mortgages were held by banks, but many more were placed by specialised mortgage brokers [Bogue, 1955]. Banks were a vital link in the web of credit, but not all credit went through organised financial markets, and not all organised financial markets worked through banks.

Taking all the financial markets together for the moment, we can test how well they did their job by looking at interest-rate differentials. A perfect capital market would have equalised interest rates throughout the country, so that a person could borrow on the same terms anywhere in the country. This manifestly was not the case in the nineteenth century. Interest rates approached a common level in the latter part of the century, but they were always higher in the West and South than in New England and the Middle Atlantic states [Davis, 1965]. Since the differences we observe were differences in quoted rates, it may be that the differences were reflections of differences in the types of loans demanded in different regions. But this hypothesis, although possible, appears implausible owing to the difficulty of specifying just how loans in different regions differed from each other. We therefore ask why interest rates differed across the country.

For the early part of the nineteenth century, communications and transportation were sufficiently slow and difficult to make it unreasonable to expect interest rates to have been equalised. There were more potential lenders relative to potential borrowers in the East than in the West, and the task of putting a western borrower

50

in contact – even indirectly – with an eastern lender was not trivial. The question becomes more interesting in the late nineteenth century, when the introduction of the railroad and the telegraph had substantially lowered these transactions costs. Sylla [1969] suggested that the high interest rates of the West under the National Banking System were the results of the design of that system. A substantial minimum capital was required to start a national bank, and this capital was hard to accumulate in a single place in the rural West. The resultant scarcity of banks in the West gave rise to local monopolies and consequently to higher interest rates. This suggestion ignores the state banks, which continued to exist even though they were no longer banks of issue. Did they offset the national banks' monopolies? Or were they ineffective competition in the absence of note issue? We do not yet know.

Ransom and Sutch [1972] made a similar case about the South, arguing that the high rate of illiteracy in the South raised the operating costs of southern banks and reduced their number. In fact, they argue that banks were bypassed by southern merchants who extended credit directly to farmers. The high interest rates of the South were then the reflection of the monopoly power of these merchants. This is a traditional argument in new clothing, but there are still some problems with it. The holders of monopoly power should be getting rich from their power, but we read more often of the failures of merchants than of their riches. In addition, the subsidiary hypothesis that the merchants enforced their monopoly power by 'locking-in' farmers to the production of cotton has been refuted [DeCanio, 1973]. The question must still be regarded as open.

Differences in interest rates have long-run effects; bank suspensions have short-run impacts. The largest peacetime banking crisis of the nineteenth century occurred at the end of the 1830s. Although it was intimately connected with the demise of the Second Bank of the United States, the crisis was induced by the refusal of the Bank of England to continue financing the expansion of Anglo-American trade. The subsequent deflation was not a necessary result of the crisis itself; it was a response to the cessation of British lending to the United States. These dramatic events had important financial and political repercussions, but they do not seem to have had much impact on the level of employment or the rate of economic growth in the United States [Temin, 1969].

The 1870s witnessed another major banking crisis and deflation. Yet the rate of growth of the economy appears to have been extraordinarily rapid in this decade [Gallman, 1966]. After a long period of deflation, there were major financial troubles again in the 1890s. This is the first financial panic in which the economy as a whole seems to have suffered major dislocation [Lebergott, 1964].

The growth of the banking system clearly encouraged American economic growth. It did not do a perfect job, as is attested by the incentives for fraud and the continued inter-regional differences in interest rates. But the economy did not suffer greatly during its periodic panics. And one can argue convincingly that the nineteenth-century banking system had the substantial result of avoiding major depressions like that of the 1930s [Friedman and Schwartz, 1963].

7 Slavery

THE institution of slavery is a problem for all American historians. There are so many questions that can be asked about this institution and so many emotions capable of being aroused by these questions that the literature is more than normally confused. Before we approach the question of slavery and economic growth, therefore, we have to clear away some of these confusions. BEGAN (17
ENDC(19

Slavery in North America began in the seventeenth century and ended in the nineteenth. Approximately half a million slaves were imported into the area that became the United States before the international slave trade was outlawed in 1808. In the southern states – the region to which slavery was largely confined – slaves constituted one-third of the population from 1790 to 1860 despite the cessation of new supplies of slaves from overseas [U.S. Bureau of the Census, 1960, *12*]. The rate of increase of the slave population in the absence of imports was the same as the rate of increase of the southern free population.

Slaves were used primarily in agriculture; and slave agriculture, on the eve of the Civil War, meant above all cotton plantations. The rise of cotton, however, was a nineteenth-century phenomenon. The innovations of the English Industrial Revolution vastly increased the demand for cotton, and Eli Whitney's invention of the cotton gin in the 1790s dramatically lowered the cost of supplying it. Southern agriculture was transformed as a result. Slaves had been used to grow tobacco, rice and sugar in the eighteenth century. While production of all these crops continued, they faded in importance as employers of slave labour.

Recent studies of the economics of American slavery have concentrated on the nineteenth century and on the production of cotton. Several different questions have been asked in the course of this recent work, of which four can be distinguished for the purposes of this discussion :

1. Would slavery have continued to be 'viable' in the American South if there had been no Civil War?
2. Was slavery profitable to slave owners?
3. How much were slaves 'exploited' by the slave owners?
4. And, finally, what was the effect of slavery on the economic development of the South and the United States as a whole?

The issue of 'viability' was raised in its modern form by Conrad and Meyer [1958] in an article that must be considered the pioneer article of the New Economic History. Conrad and Meyer asked if slavery would have 'toppled of its own weight' in the absence of the Civil War. They proposed to answer this question by examining the profitability of slavery, i.e. by answering the second question listed above. But it is clear that the profitability and viability of slavery are separate and that the relationship between them must be elucidated before inferences can be made about one from evidence on the other.

How could slavery have ended in the absence of the Civil War? The question is not how many slaves there would have been or what slave prices would have been. It has nothing to do with the characteristics of slavery if the institution of slavery had continued. It is rather a question about the demise of the institution itself. And there seem to be several possible answers. There might have been a rebellion, as in Haiti. There might have been legal emancipation without war, as in the British Empire. Slaves might all have bought their freedom from their owners, or their owners – all of them together – might have freed them without payment. Slaves might have failed to reproduce themselves, and the slave population could have dwindled until it either vanished or one of the other possibilities was initiated by the population decline. And there may be other ways for the institution to have been terminated as well.

Not all of these possibilities seem to fit the idea of slavery toppling of its own weight. Rebellion does not seem to be contemplated, either because of optimism or because of a view of the slave personality in the United States. Legal emancipation similarly does not seem to be at issue, suggesting that the question of viability does not concern the Civil War alone, but rather *all* government intervention. This suggestion cannot be accepted, however, because the possibility of slaves purchasing their freedom is not envisaged precisely because of legal restrictions on this process imposed by the state governments. The question at issue therefore seems to concern the future of slavery in the absence of interference by the federal government – or at least of federal intervention in addition to the constitutional ban on the international slave trade – but not in the absence of state laws. The interest of such a restricted question can only be assessed by an appreciation of the probable political realities in a world in which the Civil War did not take place.

Even this restricted question does not seem to be closely related to profitability. Consider the possible motives for slave owners to free their slaves. They might have done so because their profits from growing cotton with the aid of slaves were not as large as in alternative operations. But they might have freed their slaves despite the profitability of using them to grow cotton if, for example, the moral revulsion to slavery came to outweigh the financial gain. Alternatively, they might not have freed the slaves even if growing cotton was unprofitable because they might have found other occupations for them or even kept them as people keep pets or paintings – because they liked owning them. Profitability therefore is neither a necessary nor a sufficient condition for slave owners to have freed their slaves.

It must be remembered, too, that *all* slave owners must free their slaves if slavery as an institution is to vanish. If only some slave owners free their slaves, there will be fewer slaves, but the institution will continue. And if only some slave owners wish to rid themselves of slaves, they may decide to sell them to people who disagree with them, thereby avoiding a financial loss and eliminating even this small effect on slavery.

However fascinating it may be to economists to calculate profitability, it therefore must be admitted that knowledge of the profitability of slavery gives only a limited amount of knowledge about its viability. In addition, knowing whether slavery would have toppled of its own weight gives only limited clues about the necessity of fighting the Civil War in order to free the slaves. Some information is gained, because slavery was probably rendered more viable by its profitability, since it allowed people who had no particular attachment to slaves in and of themselves to purchase slaves for the profits that could be earned through them. And the suggestion that slavery was not about to topple of its own weight implies in turn that some governmental action probably would have been needed to terminate slavery in the United States, whether taken in wartime or not.

The profitability of slavery has been measured in various ways as different authors have tested the conclusions of Conrad and Meyer by using either alternative theoretical formulations of the problem or alternative data [Evans, 1962; Saraydar, 1964; Sutch, 1965]. The general result from these experiments has been to confirm Conrad and Meyer's result: it was approximately as profitable to own slaves as it was to own shares in an established firm in an established industry like the cotton-textile industry.

③ Since these findings cannot be interpreted as showing the viability of slavery, they have been used to infer something about the attitudes of slave owners toward owning slaves. Assume, to start with, that slave owners are interested in profits, but that they do not like to own slaves. Then they would choose not to make their profits by owning slaves if they could make the same profits in other ways. If they made more profits from owning slaves than from owning cotton mills, this would help to overcome their reluctance to do so, and we may presume that there is some rate of profit at which the potential slave owners would feel themselves compensated for the onus of owning slaves. Similarly, if slave owners liked having slaves for reasons other than the profits they generated, then these slave owners would be willing to hold slaves even though the profits from their activities was below the profits attainable from an equal investment in cotton mills.

The profitability of slavery therefore appears to measure the attitude of slave owners. A low profit rate means that slave owners liked owning slaves for reasons independent of profits, and a high profit rate means that they disliked owning slaves. A market rate of return, such as Conrad and Meyer found, seems to indicate that slave owners were indifferent between slaves and cotton mills as investments; they made the decisions on economic grounds alone.

56

This inference is unacceptable on two grounds [Woodman, 1972]:

1. The profitability being measured is the rate of return from current operations alone. It takes no account of the possible capital gains from owning slaves. If prices were expected to rise, then the profitability estimated by Conrad and Meyer underestimates the profits expected by slave owners holding slaves because it ignores the expected capital gains from owning slaves. If slave owners expected the slaves to be freed without compensation – whether in a civil war or not – then the measured profit overestimates the expected returns because it ignores the capital loss that such an emancipation would impose on slave owners.

If we had independent evidence on price expectations of slave owners, this would not be a problem. We could estimate the expected profits including capital gains, and make inferences from that. In the absence of such evidence, we can only make assumptions about these expectations. But the inferences about slave owners' attitudes toward slavery are only as reliable as the assumptions. Conrad and Meyer, viewed from this point of view, implicitly assumed that the prices of slaves were not expected to change in the years around 1850, an assumption that ignores both the contemporary upward trend of slave prices and the possible risk of civil war. Alternatively, we could make assumptions about slave owners' attitudes toward slavery and infer from the data what their price expectations must have been [Fogel and Engerman, 1974]. This procedure clearly is no better than the underlying assumptions about the slave owners' attitudes, assumptions that cannot be supported by profitability data since these data are now being used as indicators of other attitudes.

2. Even if we had data on price expectations, however, we still could not infer the attitudes of individual slave owners by examining the market price. The second reason for not accepting the inference from profitability to attitude is that you can never establish individual attitudes by means of market variables. If you know the attitudes of individuals, you can derive conclusions about the market. But you cannot reason the other way. How do we know that the slave owners did not want to maximise profits at all? Suppose that they liked to own slaves for non-economic

reasons. Then, since they owned slaves, they decided to work them hard enough to earn a reasonable return on their investment. We would observe the normal rate of return found by Conrad and Meyer, but we would not be able to infer that the slave owners lacked a non-economic desire to own slaves. Similarly, if a higher (or lower) profit rate had been observed, that might indicate only that the market rate was too easily earned (or was unattainable) by slave owners holding slaves for reasons unrelated to profits.

The literature on the profitability of slavery therefore yields only meagre conclusions. We can conclude that it was possible for slave owners to earn a market rate of return from owning slaves, because they did it. We can infer further *either* that they did not have non-economic motives for owning slaves *or* that they did not have both the ability and the desire to work slaves harder than they did. These are different conclusions from those Conrad and Meyer were seeking when they initiated the modern discussion of profitability, but they are hardly without interest.

The third question that has been asked of slavery is quite different from the first two. An attempt to measure the degree of 'exploitation' of slaves turns away from the questions of prediction and motivation discussed above toward the implications of slavery for the slaves. Everyone agrees that slavery was not a desirable condition for the slaves; a measure of 'exploitation' is an attempt to provide an index of just how bad the condition was.

Engerman introduced this concept into the discussion of American slavery in the following way. 'A positive price for a new-born [slave] infant meant that . . . the expected value of lifetime output exceeded the expected costs of raising and maintaining the slave until death. . . . The positive price for an infant therefore provides an estimate of the discounted value of expected exploitation of the slave' [Engerman, 1973, *47*]. This is very much an economist's view of exploitation. It measures the difference between what the slave produces (his output) and what he is 'paid' (his maintenance). It is based on the presumption that each person is entitled to a wage equal to his marginal product, which is what it would be in a world of perfect competition. There are other income distributions that might furnish a superior normative standard, such as an equal distribution among the population. The distribution of income under slavery could be compared to each of these distributions to derive different measures of the degree of exploitation. There will be as many different measures of exploitation as there are distributions of income that historians find desirable.

One can also define exploitation without reference to income. Assume for the moment that slaves were paid their marginal product. Under the definition of exploitation introduced by Engerman, they would not have been exploited. But they could have been 'exploited' under this assumption by being made to work harder or longer than they would have chosen to do had they been free. The 'exploitation' would have consisted in the slaves' inability to enjoy the leisure that they would have chosen to enjoy at the prevailing wage. We know that freedmen and particularly freedwomen worked fewer hours after the Civil War than they had before the war. This change could be used to get a measure of 'exploitation' quite different from any of those based on wage rates.

The difference between these two classes of definitions of exploitation – one based on earnings and the other on hours worked – can be seen in another way. Assume that slave owners were profit maximisers, that they had full control over slave fertility, that they operated a slave-breeding industry, and that this industry was in long-run equilibrium. (These assumptions are presented for the sake of argument; no presumption is implied about their historical relevance.) The value of a new-born slave would then be equal to the cost of producing the baby, which would be simply the cost of having the mother out of the cotton fields for a few months. The price of a slave infant would also be equal to the difference between the discounted value of the slave's future productivity and the discounted value of the slave's future earnings. In other words, the rate of exploitation as defined by Engerman would be equal to the cost of removing a female slave from the fields for a few months. Since this is a small number relative to the lifetime earnings of a slave, the degree of exploitation under this definition would be small. Yet no one would want to say that under these assumptions slaves were not exploited or that they were exploited 'only a little'. Under a definition of exploitation that measured the exploitation by the divergence between the slaves' actual lives and the lives they would have chosen to live if free, the degree of exploitation under these assumptions could be very large indeed.

This brief discussion of exploitation gives only a glimpse at a few of the many issues raised by the introduction of this emotionally-charged term. Problems of the measurement itself, for example, have not been mentioned. Nor has the possibility of non-economic exploitation, like sexual exploitation. These and other issues were discussed at length by Fogel and Engerman [1974]. (Their methods have been analysed critically by David and Temin [1974].)

Having shown some of the complexities in the discussion of American slavery, we can now turn to the effect of this institution on economic growth. It should be clear from the discussion of the railroads in a previous chapter that the effect of the existence of slavery on economic growth cannot be measured by simply looking at the private profitability of slavery. This is a question about the economy as a whole, and it need bear no relation to the experiences of any single individual or single group within the economy. We therefore must shift our focus from the specific master–slave relationship to the southern economy as a whole.

One strand of this argument points to the effect of slavery on the distribution of income and skills in the South. Slaves were poor and illiterate; this must have retarded economic growth [Genovese, 1962]. Despite the attractiveness of this argument, both halves of it must be acknowledged to be weak. An unequal distribution of income may restrict the growth of demand for consumer products. But if it does so, it must also increase the growth of savings available for investment. And in many models of economic growth, the positive effect of larger savings outweighs the negative effect of a smaller consumer demand. The role of education in economic growth has not been disputed on theoretical grounds. But the work of Abramovitz and David discussed above suggests that American economic growth may be explained quite well by the growth in the labour force and capital stock without reference to education. The effects of illiteracy in the first half of the nineteenth century may simply have been small. After all, public education in Britain was not widespread until after the end of American slavery.

Another strand of this argument starts from the concentration of southern agriculture on cotton. It is argued that the institution of slavery forced the South into an uneconomic specialisation in the cultivation of cotton. But is this true? It is possible that the South grew cotton because it had a comparative advantage in this activity, and that it would have grown cotton whether or not slavery existed. Cotton continued to be grown in the *post-bellum* South in great quantities despite the demise of slavery. And since slaves were not employed exclusively in growing cotton, the effect of slavery on the composition of output is hard to estimate. It is hard to refute the presumption that the South's concentration on cotton was largely independent of slavery [Engerman, 1967].

The southern concentration on cotton has also been seen as a good thing for the development of the United States as a whole. North [1961] argued that the rapidly rising production and export of cotton sparked off American economic growth. It provided foreign exchange; it encouraged the growth of the textile industry; it stimulated the development of financial and commercial services in the United States. North did not go so far as to say that slavery was good for the country; but to the extent that the production of cotton was facilitated by slavery, his argumen would suggest that it was.

The results of these and other influences on southern – and non-southern – growth rates can be seen in data on regional incomes compiled by Easterlin [1961]. The first three lines of Table 4 show that the South grew as rapidly as the North in the two decades before the Civil War, using per capita income as the measure of growth. (This conclusion is unaffected by the exclusion of slaves from the relevant population, as the second column of Table 4 shows.) This growth, however, may not have been the result of the same processes in the North and South. Following the method of David in his exploitation of income growth before 1840, we may decompose the growth in each region into the growth resulting from changes within sub-regions and the growth coming from the redistribution of the population between subregions. The growth of per capita incomes in northern and

Table 4

Change in Real Per Capita Income 1840–60
(Percentages)

	Total population	Free population
United States	33	32
North	29	29
South	39	43
North-east	40	41
North Central	37	36
South Atlantic	27	29
East South Central	29	35
West South Central	22	15

Source : Woodman [1972, *337*]. The data are from Easterlin, in Harris [1961], and Gallman [1966].

southern sub-regions is shown in the balance of Table 4 where it can be seen that every sub-region of the North grew more rapidly than every sub-region of the South. Growth in the North was retarded by the movement of population from the rich and industrialised East to the agricultural West. Growth in the South, by contrast, was aided by the movement of population into the fertile lands of the New South.

These figures, it must be admitted, do not clarify the issue. We can agree with Engerman [1967] that the figures for the regions taken as units are the relevant ones, or with Woodman [1972] that the figures for the sub-regions are important. The North was growing despite the development of the West; the South was growing because of it. This is a result of the different economic characteristics of the northern and southern seaboard regions, and these differences may have been at least partly the result of the existence of slavery in the South. But if the South was exploiting its comparative advantage by growing cotton, it may be questioned whether it would have been better off during the *ante bellum* period by imitating the North and promoting industrialisation. One would have to compare the relative benefits of migration and industrialisation to answer this question.

The discussion of the effect of slavery on growth in the literature has therefore served to ask this difficult question, but not yet to answer it. But it has dispelled the idea that slavery had to be inefficient because it was immoral. Slavery may have retarded the growth of the South. But if it did, the effects are hardly as apparent as a thorough-going moralist might wish.

8 Conclusion

THE British North American colonies grew in extent in the eighteenth century. This process continued into the nineteenth as the United States moved west from the Atlantic coast. The new land was more fertile than the old, and an abundance of navigable rivers permitted the products of American agriculture to be transported from the interior.

But a second, and more important, process was overlaid on this one in the course of the nineteenth century. Starting almost with the Revolution, people began to forsake agriculture for other occupations. These other occupations, to the extent that we know of them, were new ones – created by the emerging Industrial Revolution. Some of the new activities helped agriculture. The railroad offered a new and more flexible means of transporting agricultural produce, and mechanical innovations increased the productivity of farm workers. Other activities encouraged the expansion of the production of non-agricultural goods and services, an expansion that continues today.

This is a familiar story, but the research surveyed here has altered many of the details and changed some of the outlines. Intensive economic growth, we now know, started at the beginning of the nineteenth century, not near the middle. Since industry was still small at the start of the century, the workers leaving agriculture must have been going into commercial or other activities. The process of economic growth was not simply one of industrialisation.

Similarly, although the opening up of new land yielded increased output, not everyone benefited. New lands were in competition with the old, and the owners of land in the older agricultural areas seem to have suffered. Consumers – both in the United States and abroad – gained. Many people have said that the new land hurt American industry by draining away its labour force; many others have said that it helped by creating a larger market. These issues have been clarified by recent work, but the question is still open.

The growth of industry was both cause and effect of increasing technical sophistication and abilities. New machines, new methods and new products appeared continuously throughout the nineteenth century in a process of change that can be largely understood on the basis of costs and returns. To the extent that we can tell at this distance, the American economy encouraged the adoption of the most profitable technique. The general view is that the American entrepreneur took an active role in this process, but the rapidity of change in America may just have eliminated all those who did not produce in accord with market incentives – whatever any producer's motives were.

One innovation that seemed to contemporaries to combine the agricultural and industrial components of growth was the railroad. Recent work has shown that nineteenth-century paeans to the railroad's glory need to be understood as hymns, not as economic analysis. But the pendulum must not be allowed to swing too far. There is no evidence that the railroads were useless or – worse – a colossal mistake. They absorbed a large part of American investment in the second half of the nineteenth century, and the social return, if not always the private return, amply justified this expenditure.

With the growth of production went a growth of financial services. The development of American banking was colourful and occasionally dramatic. The drama, however, seems to have been largely independent of economic growth. Further, the pace of economic activity does not seem to have slackened more than briefly during the periodic crises. The growth of the banking system played a useful role in allocating resources, but the task of transferring resources from East to West was too big to be accomplished perfectly. Granted the inefficiencies of the fragmented American banking system, it is hard to think of an alternative better suited to the needs of the expanding American economy.

Slavery also seems to have had very little impact on growth. The South grew under slavery, and the production of cotton in slave plantations expanded to meet the demand. The argument that immoral institutions have to be economically inefficient is erroneous; the slaves suffered, but there is no evidence that the slave owners did too. Research continues on these questions, as historians try to define and to measure the extent of the cost of slavery to the slaves and the benefits to the owners. Moral and economic issues intertwine, and the concepts of 'cost' and 'benefit' are exceedingly problematical and complex in this context.

This survey has covered only a selection of the problems of American economic growth and of the recent literature on it. Nevertheless the way in which new work is restructuring the story can be seen. Connections between parts of the economy and between the American and British economies are being emphasised, and distinctions are being drawn between actions and institutions that were important for political or moral reasons and those that were important for economic growth. As this research continues, so will our understanding of the complex process called economic growth.

Bibliography

INTRODUCTORY NOTE

This note mentions a few important publications not noticed earlier in the text.

There are comparatively few texts embodying the results of recent research. Davis, Hughes and McDougall [1969] made perhaps the best attempt to do so in a classic textbook format. Harris [1961] and Davis *et al.* [1972] are textbooks on a different model: each chapter was written by a different scholar. The resultant gain in breadth is offset in some parts by a loss in unity, and the results are somewhere between a traditional text and an anthology.

Several anthologies of articles such as those discussed here have appeared. A small collection similar in approach to the discussion here is in Temin [1973]. A larger and more inclusive collection is in Fogel and Engerman [1971]. Other useful anthologies are Aitken [1967], Carstensen [1963], Coats and Robertson [1969], *Purdue Faculty Papers* [1967] and Scheiber [1964].

The most useful single compilation of data is in *Historical Statistics of the United States*, published by the United States Bureau of the Census [1960]. Additional useful data can be found in two volumes of the National Bureau of Economic Research conference series [1960, 1966], in the massive study of migration and related matters by Kuznets and Thomas [1957], and in a book by Lebergott [1964]. Data on the distribution of wealth at different times have been compiled by Gallman [1969], Jones [1970, 1972], and Soltow [1969, 1971]. The iron industry and the cotton industry, the two industries with the best data, have been the subjects of recent industry histories, the former by Temin [1964] and the latter by McGouldrick [1968]. Agriculture has been surveyed ably by Bogue [1963] and Danhof [1969].

Several articles on the tariff have appeared in the last few years, but they have been concerned primarily with questions regarding the specification of industry supply curves, rather than the tariff. Thus Fogel and Engerman [1969] discussed the tariff on iron in the

1840s, but they were mainly concerned with the use of *a priori* information to replace missing data on industry capacity. Similarly, David [1970] discussed the *antebellum* tariff on cotton textiles, but the main question of his paper was how to model the process of technical change and 'learning by doing.' The former article has been disputed by Joskow and McKelvey [1973]; the latter, by Williamson [1972]. David [1972] has replied to Williamson. More direct approach to questions of international trade can be found in Williamson's [1964] analysis of long swings in trade and Kravis's [1970] comparison of nineteenth- and twentieth-century trade patterns.

Government support of canals and railroads – 'internal improvements' in the language of the time – has been studied from the point of view of government policy. The question is not whether canals and railroads were good for the economy, but rather whether government action was needed to have them built and whether the policy that was actually used was the best one, evaluated from the point of view of the resulting income distribution. Goodrich [1960, 1961] and his students provided a general survey of the nineteenth century and studies of canals. Fogel [1960] and Mercer [1970] studied land grants to the railroads.

The export-base theory of economic growth has been applied to the United States by North [1961]. He argued that the production of cotton was the mainspring of American growth in the early nineteenth century, operating through a network of regional specialisation and trade. The existence of this trade has been questioned by several people who have tried to contest North's hypothesis that much of the food for the cotton-growing South was grown in the West [Fishlow, 1964; Gallman, 1970; Lindstrom, 1970].

Some recent studies have tried to answer the old question of whether immigrants were 'pushed' or 'pulled' into the United States. The approach typically has been statistical, and the results depend on the specification used [Easterlin, 1961; Wilkinson, 1970; Gallaway and Vedder, 1971; Quigley, 1972].

Engerman [1966] summarises the evidence on the economic impact of the Civil War.

SOURCES CITED

The following abbreviations are used for certain journals mentioned in the ensuing list:

A.E.R. : *American Economic Review*
E.H.R. : *Economic History Review*
E.J. : *Economic Journal*
J.E.H. : *Journal of Economic History*
J.P.E. : *Journal of Political Economy*

Abramovitz, M., and David, P., 'Reinterpreting Economic Growth: Parables and Realities', *A.E.R.*, LXIII (May 1973) *428–39*.

Aitken, H. (ed.), *Explorations in Enterprise* (Cambridge, Mass., 1967).

Bogue, A. G., *From Prairie to Corn Belt* (Chicago, 1963).

——*Money at Interest: The Farm Mortgage on the Middle Border* (Ithaca, N.Y., 1955).

Bogue, M. B., and Bogue, A. G., ' "Profits" and the Frontier Land Speculator', *J.E.H.*, XVII (March 1957) *1–24*.

Boyd, J., and Walton, G., 'The Social Savings from Nineteenth-Century Rail Passenger Services', *Explorations in Economic History*, IX (1972) *233–54*.

Cagan, P., *Determinants and Effects of Changes in the Stock of Money, 1875–1960* (National Bureau of Economic Research, New York, 1965).

Carstensen, V. (ed.), *The Public Lands* (Madison, Wis., 1963).

Coats, A. W., and Robertson, R. M. (eds), *Essays in American Economic History* (London, 1969).

Cochren, T. C., 'Did the Civil War Retard Industrialization?', *Mississippi Valley Historical Review*, XLVIII (September 1961) *191–210*.

Conrad, A. H., and Meyer, J. R., 'The Economics of Slavery in the Antebellum South', *J.P.E.*, LXVI (April 1958) *95–130*.

Danhof, C. H., *Change in Agriculture* (Cambridge, Mass., 1969).

David, P. A., 'The Mechanization of Reaping in the Ante-bellum Midwest', in *Industrialisation in Two Systems: Essays in Honor of Alexander Gerschenkron*, ed. H. Rosovsky (New York, 1966) *3–39*.

——, 'The Growth of Real Product in the United States before 1840: New Evidence, Controlled Conjectures', *J.E.H.*, XXVII (June 1967) *151–97*.

——, 'Transport Innovation and Economic Growth: Professor Fogel on and off the Rails', *E.H.R.*, second series, XXII (December 1969) *506–25*.

——, 'Learning by Doing and Tariff Protection: A Reconsideration of the Case of the Ante-bellum United States Cotton Textile Industry', *J.E.H.*, XXX (September 1970) *521–601*.

——, 'The Use and Abuse of Prior Information in Econometric History: A Rejoinder to Professor Williamson on the Ante-bellum Cotton Textile Industry', *J.E.H.*, xxxii (September 1972) *706–27*.

David, P. A., and Temin, P., 'Slavery: the Progressive Institution?', *J. E. H.*, xxxiv (September 1974) *739–83*.

Davis, L. E., 'Stock Ownership in the Early New England Textile Industry', *Business History Review*, xxxii (1958) *204–22*.

——, [1965], 'The Investment Market, 1870–1914: The Evolution of a National Market', *J.E.H.*, xxv (September 1965) *355–99*.

Davis, L. E., Hughes, J. R. T., and McDougall, D. M., *American Economic History*, 3rd ed. (Homewood, Ill., 1969).

Davis, L. E., *et al.*, *American Economic Growth* (New York, 1972).

DeCanio, S., 'Cotton "Overproduction" in Late Nineteenth-Century Southern Agriculture', *J.E.H.*, xxxiii (September, 1973) *608–33*.

Diamond, S., 'Values as an Obstacle to Economic Growth: The American Colonies', *J.E.H.*, xxvii (December 1967) *561–75*.

Easterlin, R. A., 'Regional Income Trends, 1840–1950', in *American Economic History*, ed. S. E. Harris (New York 1961) *525–47*.

——, 'The American Population', ch. 5 in L. E. Davis *et al.* (1972) (see above).

Engerman, S. L., 'The Economic Impact of the Civil War', *Explorations in Entrepreneurial History*, second series, iii (1966) *176–99*.

——, 'The Effects of Slavery upon the Southern Economy: A Review of the Recent Debate', *Explorations in Entrepreneurial History*, second series, ii (1967) *71–97*.

——, 'Some Considerations relating to Property Rights in Man', *J.E.H.*, xxxiii (March 1973) *43–65*.

Evans, R., Jr, 'The Economics of American Negro Slavery', *Aspects of Labor Economics* (National Bureau of Economic Research, New York, 1962).

Feller, I., 'The Draper Loom in New England Textiles, 1894–1914: A Study of Diffusion of an Innovation', *J.E.H.*, xxvi (September 1966) *320–47*.

Fenichel, A. H., 'Growth and Diffusion of Power in Manufacturing, 1838–1919', in *Output, Employment, and Productivity in the United States after 1800* (1966) (see under National Bureau) *443–78*.

Fisher, F. M., and Temin, P., 'Regional Specialisation and the Supply of Wheat in the U.S., 1867–1914', *Review of Economics and Statistics*, lii (May 1970) *134–49*.

Fishlow, A., 'Antebellum and Interregional Trade Reconsidered',

A.E.R., LIV (May 1964) *352–76*.

——, *American Railroads and the Transformation of the Antebellum Economy* (Cambridge, Mass., 1965).

——, 'Productivity and Technological Change in the Railroad Sector, 1840–1910', in *Output, Employment, and Productivity in the United States after 1800* (1966) (see under National Bureau), *583–646*.

Fogel, R. W., *The Union Pacific Railroad: A Case in Premature Enterprise* (Baltimore, 1960).

——, 'A Quantitative Approach to the Study of Railroads in American Economic Growth: A Report of Some Preliminary Findings', *J.E.H.*, XXII (June 1962) *163–97*.

——, *Railroads and American Economic Growth: Essays in Econometric History* (Baltimore, 1964).

——, 'Railroads as an Analogy to the Space Effort: Some Economic Aspects', *E.J.*, LXXVI (March 1966).

——, 'The Specification Problem in Economic History', *J.E.H.*, XXVII (September 1967) *283–308*.

Fogel, R. W., and Engerman, S. L., 'A Model for the Explanation of Industrial Expansion during the Nineteenth Century: With an Application to the American Iron Industry', *J.P.E.* LXXVII (May 1969) *306–28*.

—— (eds), *The Reinterpretation of American Economic History* (New York, 1971).

——, *Time on the Cross* (Boston, Mass., 1974).

Friedman, M., and Schwartz, A. J., *A Monetary History of the United States, 1867–1960* (Princeton, N. J., 1963).

Gallaway, L. E. and Vedder, R. K., 'Emigration from the United Kingdom to the United States: 1860–1913', *J.E.H.* XXXI (December 1971) *885–97*.

Gallman, R. E., 'Gross National Product in the United States, 1834–1909', in *Output, Employment, and Productivity in the United States after 1800* (1966) (see under National Bureau), *3–76*.

——, 'Trends in the Size Distribution of Wealth in the Nineteenth Century: Some Speculations', in *Six Papers on the Size Distribution of Wealth and Income*, ed. L. Soltow (National Bureau of Economic Research, New York, 1969) *1–30*.

——, 'Self-Sufficiency in the Cotton Economy of the Antebellum South', in *The Structure of the Cotton Economy of the Antebellum South*, ed. W. N. Parker (Agricultural History Society, Washington D.C., 1970) *5–23*.

Genovese, E. D., 'The Significance of the Slave Plantation for Southern Economic Development', *Journal of Southern History*, XXVII (1962) *422–37*.

Gilchrist, D. T., and Lewis, W. D. (eds), *Economic Change in the Civil War Era* (Greenville, Del., 1965).

Goodrich, C., *Government Promotion of American Canals and Railroads, 1800–1890* (New York, 1960).

——(ed.), *Canals and American Economic Development* (New York, 1961).

Habakkuk, H. J., *American and British Technology in the Nineteenth Century* (Cambridge, 1962).

Hammond, B., *Banks and Politics in America from the Revolution to the Civil War* (Princeton, N.J., 1957).

——, *Sovereignty and an Empty Purse: Banks and Politics in the Civil War* (Princeton, N.J., 1970).

Harris, S. E. (ed.), *American Economic History* (New York, 1961).

Hawke, G. R., *Railways and Economic Growth in England and Wales, 1840–1870* (Oxford, 1970).

Jones, A. H., 'Wealth Estimates for the American Middle Colonies, 1774', *Economic Development and Cultural Change*, XVII (July 1970) Part 2.

——, 'Wealth Estimates for the New England Colonies about 1770', *J.E.H.*, XXXII (March 1972) *98–127*.

Joskow, P. L., and McKelvey, E. F., 'The Fogel–Engerman Iron Model: A Clarifying Note', *J.P.E.*, LXXXI (September/October, 1973) *1236–40*.

Kravis, I., 'Trade as a Handmaiden of Growth: Similarities between Nineteenth and Twentieth Centuries', *E.J.*, LXXX (December 1970) *850–72*.

Kuznets, S. (ed.), *Income and Wealth of the United States: Trends and Structure*, Income and Wealth, Series II (Cambridge, England, 1952).

Kuznets, S., and Thomas, D. S. (eds), *Population Distribution and Economic Growth, United States 1870–1950* (American Philosophical Society, Philadelphia, 1957) 3 vols.

Lebergott, S., *Manpower in Economic Growth: The United States Record since 1800* (New York, 1964).

——, 'United States Transport Advance and Externalities', *J.E.H.*, XXVI (December 1966) *437–61*.

Lindstrom, D. L., 'Southern Dependence on Interregional Grain Supplies: A Review of the Trade Flows, 1840–1860', in *The*

Structure of the Cotton Economy of the Antebellum South, ed. W. N. Parker (Agricultural History Society, Washington D.C., 1970) *101–13*.

Martin, R. F., *National Income in the United States, 1799–1938* (National Industrial Conference Board, New York, 1939).

Matthews, R. C. O., *A Study in Trade-Cycle History: Economic Fluctuations in Great Britain, 1833–42* (Cambridge, England, 1954).

McClelland, P. D., 'Railroads, American Growth, and the New Economic History: A Critique', *J.E.H.*, xxviii (March 1968) *102–23*.

——, 'Social Rates of Return on American Railroads in the Nineteenth Century', *E.H.R.*, second series xxv (August 1972) *471–88*.

McGouldrick, P. F., *New England Textiles in the Nineteenth Century: Profits and Investment* (Cambridge, Mass., 1968).

Mercer, L. J., 'Rates of Return for Land-Grant Railroads: The Central Pacific System', *J.E.H.*, xxx (September 1970) *602–26*.

National Bureau of Economic Research, *Trends in the American Economy in the Nineteenth Century* (Princeton, N.J., 1960).

——, *Output, Employment, and Productivity in the United States after 1800* (New York, 1966).

Nerlove, M. [1966], 'Railroads and American Economic Growth', *J.E.H.*, xxvi (March 1966) *107–15*.

North, D.C., *The Economic Growth of the United States, 1790–1860* (Englewood Cliffs, N.J., 1961).

Parker, W. N., and Klein, J. L. V., 'Productivity Growth in Grain Production in the United States, 1840–60 and 1900–10', in *Output, Employment, and Productivity in the United States after 1800* (see under National Bureau) *523–82*.

Parker, W. N., and Whartenby, F., 'The Growth of Output before 1840', in *Trends in the American Economy in the Nineteenth Century* (see under National Bureau) *191–212*.

Passell, P., 'The Impact of Cotton Land Distribution on the Antebellum Economy', *J.E.H.*, xxi *917–37.*(December 1971)

Passell, P., and Schmundt, M., 'Pre-Civil War Land Policy and the Growth of Manufacturing', *Explorations in Economic History*, ix (1971) *35–48*.

Passell, P., and Wright, G., 'Effects of pre-Civil War Territorial Expansion on the Price of Slaves', *J.P.E.*, lxxx (November 1972) *1188–1202*.

Pollard, S., 'Fixed Capital in the Industrial Revolution in Britain',

J.E.H., xxiv (September 1964) *299–314*.

Purdue Faculty Papers in Economic History, 1956–1966, Homewood, Ill., 1967).

Quigley, J. M., An Economic Model of Swedish Emigration,' *Quarterly Journal of Economics*, lxxxvi (February 1972) *111–26*.

Ransom, R. L., 'Canals and Development: A Discussion of the Issues', *A.E.R.*, liv (May 1964) *356–76*.

——, 'Social Returns from Public Transport Investment: A Case Study of the Ohio Canal', *J.P.E.*, lxxviii (September 1970) *1041–60*.

Ransom, R. L., and Sutch, R., 'Debt Peonage in the Cotton South after the Civil War', *J.E.H.*, xxxii (September 1972) *641–69*.

Rosenberg, N., *Technology and American Economic Growth* (New York, 1972).

Rostow, W. W., *The Stages of Economic Growth* (Cambridge, England, 1960).

Saraydar, E., 'A Note on the Profitability of Antebellum Slavery', *Southern Economic Journal*, xxx (1964) *325–32*.

Scheiber, H. N. (ed.), *United States Economic History: Selected Readings* (New York, 1964).

Sharkey, R. P., *Money, Class, and Party: An Economic Study of Civil War and Reconstruction* (Baltimore, 1959).

Solow, R. M., *Growth Theory: An Exposition* (Oxford, 1970).

Soltow, L. C., 'Evidence on Income Inequality in the United States, 1866–1965', *J.E.H.*, xxix (June 1969) *279–86*.

——, *Patterns of Wealth-holding in Wisconsin since 1850* (Madison, Wis., 1971).

Sutch, R., 'The Profitability of Antebellum Slavery: Revisited'. *Southern Economic Journal*, xxxi (1965) *365–77*.

Swierenga, R. P., 'Land Speculator "Profits" Reconsidered: Central Iowa as a Test Case', *J.E.H.*, xxvi (March 1966) *1–28*.

Sylla, R., 'Federal Policy, Banking Market Structure, and Capital Mobilisation in the United States, 1863–1913', *J.E.H.*, xxix (December 1969) *657–86*.

Taylor, G. R., *The Transportation Revolution, 1815–1860* (New York, 1951).

Temin, P., *Iron and Steel in Nineteenth Century America: An Economic Inquiry* (Cambridge, Mass., 1964).

——, 'Steam and Waterpower in the Early Nineteenth Century', *J.E.H.*, xxvi (June 1966 *a*) *187–205*.

——, 'Labor Scarcity and the Problem of American Industrial

Efficiency in the 1850s', *J.E.H.*, xxvi (September 1966 *b*) *277–98*.
——, *The Jacksonian Economy* (New York, 1969).
——, 'Labor Scarcity in America', *Journal of Interdisciplinary History*, i (Winter 1971) *251–64*.
—— (ed.), *New Economic History* (Harmondsworth, Middlesex, 1973).
United States Bureau of the Census, *Historical Statistics of the United States: Colonial Times to 1957* (Washington, D.C., 1960).
Van Fenstermaker, J., *The Development of American Commerical Banking, 1772–1837* (Kent, Ohio, 1965).
Walton, G. M., 'A Measure of Productivity Change in American Colonial Shipping', *E.H.R.*, second series, xxi (August 1968) *268–82*.
Wilkinson, M., 'European Migration in the United States: An Econometric Analysis of Aggregate Labor Supply and Demand', *Review of Economics and Statistics*, lii (1970) *272–9*.
Williamson, J. G., *American Growth and the Balance of Payments, 1820–1913* (Chapel Hill, N. Carolina, 1964).
——, 'Embodiment, Disembodiment, Learning by Doing, and Returns to Scale in Nineteenth-Century Cotton Textiles', *J.E.H.*, xxxii (September 1972) *691–705*.
Woodman, H. D., 'Economic History and Economic Theory: The New Economic History in America', *Journal of Interdisciplinary History*, iii (Autumn 1972).
Wright, G., 'An Econometric Study of Cotton Production and Trade, 1830–1860', *Review of Economics and Statistics*, liii (May 1971) *111–20*.
Zevin, R. B., 'The Growth of Cotton Textile Production after 1815', in *The Reinterpretation of American Economic History*, ed. R. W. Fogel and S. L. Engerman (New York, 1971) *122–47*.

Index